AI
Self-Driving Cars
Accordance

Practical Advances in
Artificial Intelligence and Machine Learning

Dr. Lance B. Eliot, MBA, PhD

DEDICATION

To my incredible daughter, Lauren, and my incredible son, Michael.

Forest fortuna adiuvat (from the Latin; good fortune favors the brave).

CONTENTS

Dr. Lance B. Eliot

ACKNOWLEDGMENTS

I have been the beneficiary of advice and counsel by many friends, colleagues, family, investors, and many others. I want to thank everyone that has aided me throughout my career. I write from the heart and the head, having experienced first-hand what it means to have others around you that support you during the good times and the tough times.

To Warren Bennis, one of my doctoral advisors and ultimately a colleague, I offer my deepest thanks and appreciation, especially for his calm and insightful wisdom and support.

To Mark Stevens and his generous efforts toward funding and supporting the USC Stevens Center for Innovation.

To Lloyd Greif and the USC Lloyd Greif Center for Entrepreneurial Studies for their ongoing encouragement of founders and entrepreneurs.

To Peter Drucker, William Wang, Aaron Levie, Peter Kim, Jon Kraft, Cindy Crawford, Jenny Ming, Steve Milligan, Chis Underwood, Frank Gehry, Buzz Aldrin, Steve Forbes, Bill Thompson, Dave Dillon, Alan Fuerstman, Larry Ellison, Jim Sinegal, John Sperling, Mark Stevenson, Anand Nallathambi, Thomas Barrack, Jr., and many other innovators and leaders that I have met and gained mightily from doing so.

Thanks to Ed Trainor, Kevin Anderson, James Hickey, Wendell Jones, Ken Harris, DuWayne Peterson, Mike Brown, Jim Thornton, Abhi Beniwal, Al Biland, John Nomura, Eliot Weinman, John Desmond, and many others for their unwavering support during my career.

And most of all thanks as always to Lauren and Michael, for their ongoing support and for having seen me writing and heard much of this material during the many months involved in writing it. To their patience and willingness to listen.

Dr. Lance B. Eliot

INTRODUCTION

This is a book that provides the newest innovations and the latest Artificial Intelligence (AI) advances about the emerging nature of AI-based autonomous self-driving driverless cars. Via recent advances in Artificial Intelligence (AI) and Machine Learning (ML), we are nearing the day when vehicles can control themselves and will not require and nor rely upon human intervention to perform their driving tasks (or, that <u>allow</u> for human intervention, but only *require* human intervention in very limited ways).

Similar to my other related books, which I describe in a moment and list the chapters in the Appendix A of this book, I am particularly focused on those advances that pertain to self-driving cars. The phrase "autonomous vehicles" is often used to refer to any kind of vehicle, whether it is ground-based or in the air or sea, and whether it is a cargo hauling trailer truck or a conventional passenger car. Though the aspects described in this book are certainly applicable to all kinds of autonomous vehicles, I am focused more so here on cars.

Indeed, I am especially known for my role in aiding the advancement of self-driving cars, serving currently as the Executive Director of the Cybernetic AI Self-Driving Cars Institute. In addition to writing software, designing and developing systems and software for self-driving cars, I also speak and write quite a bit about the topic. This book is a collection of some of my more advanced essays. For those of you that might have seen my essays posted elsewhere, I have updated them and integrated them into this book as one handy cohesive package.

You might be interested in companion books that I have written that provide additional key innovations and fundamentals about self-driving cars. Those books are entitled **"Introduction to Driverless Self-Driving Cars," "Advances in AI and Autonomous Vehicles: Cybernetic Self-Driving Cars," "Self-Driving Cars: "The Mother of All AI Projects," "Innovation and Thought Leadership on Self-Driving Driverless Cars," "New Advances in AI Autonomous Driverless Self-Driving Cars," "Autonomous Vehicle Driverless Self-Driving Cars and Artificial Intelligence," "Transformative Artificial Intelligence Driverless Self-Driving Cars," "Disruptive Artificial Intelligence and Driverless Self-Driving Cars, and "State-of-the-Art AI Driverless Self-Driving Cars," and "Top Trends in AI Self-Driving Cars," and "AI Innovations and Self-Driving Cars," "Crucial Advances for AI**

Driverless Cars," "Sociotechnical Insights and AI Driverless Cars," "Pioneering Advances for AI Driverless Cars" and "Leading Edge Trends for AI Driverless Cars," "The Cutting Edge of AI Autonomous Cars" and "The Next Wave of AI Self-Driving Cars" and "Revolutionary Innovations of AI Self-Driving Cars," and "AI Self-Driving Cars Breakthroughs," "Trailblazing Trends for AI Self-Driving Cars," "Ingenious Strides for AI Driverless Cars," "AI Self-Driving Cars Inventiveness," "Visionary Secrets of AI Driverless Cars," "Spearheading AI Self-Driving Cars," "Spurring AI Self-Driving Cars," "Avant-Garde AI Driverless Cars," "AI Self-Driving Cars Evolvement," "AI Driverless Cars Chrysalis," "Boosting AI Autonomous Cars," "AI Self-Driving Cars Trendsetting," "AI Autonomous Cars Forefront, "AI Autonomous Cars Emergence," "AI Autonomous Cars Progress," "AI Self-Driving Cars Prognosis," "AI Self-Driving Cars Momentum," "AI Self-Driving Cars Headway," "AI Self-Driving Cars Vicissitude," "AI Self-Driving Cars Autonomy," "AI Driverless Cars Transmutation," "AI Driverless Cars Potentiality," "AI Driverless Cars Realities," "AI Self-Driving Cars Materiality, "AI Self-Driving Cars Accordance" (they are available on Amazon).

For this book, I am going to borrow my introduction from those companion books, since it does a good job of laying out the landscape of self-driving cars and my overall viewpoints on the topic.

INTRODUCTION TO SELF-DRIVING CARS

This is a book about self-driving cars. Someday in the future, we'll all have self-driving cars and this book will perhaps seem antiquated, but right now, we are at the forefront of the self-driving car wave. Daily news bombards us with flashes of new announcements by one car maker or another and leaves the impression that within the next few weeks or maybe months that the self-driving car will be here. A casual non-technical reader would assume from these news flashes that in fact we must be on the cusp of a true self-driving car.

We are still quite a distance from having a true self-driving car.

A true self-driving car is akin to a moonshot. In the same manner that getting us to the moon was an incredible feat, likewise, is achieving a true self-driving car. Anybody that suggests or even brashly states that the true self-driving car is nearly here should be viewed with great skepticism. Indeed, you'll see that I often tend to use the word "hogwash" or "crock" when I assess much of the decidedly *fake news* about self-driving cars.

Indeed, I've been writing a popular blog post about self-driving cars and hitting hard on those that try to wave their hands and pretend that we are on the imminent verge of true self-driving cars. For many years, I've been known as the AI Insider. Besides writing about AI, I also develop AI software. I do what I describe. It also gives me insights into what others that are doing AI are really doing versus what it is said they are doing.

Many faithful readers had asked me to pull together my insightful short essays and put them into another book, which you are now holding.

For those of you that have been reading my essays over the years, this collection not only puts them together into one handy package, I also updated the essays and added new material. For those of you that are new to the topic of self-driving cars and AI, I hope you find these essays approachable and informative. I also tend to have a writing style with a bit of a voice, and so you'll see that I am times have a wry sense of humor and poke at conformity.

As a former professor and founder of an AI research lab, I for many years wrote in the formal language of academic writing. I published in referred journals and served as an editor for several AI journals. This writing here is not of the nature, and I have adopted a different and more informal style for these essays. That being said, I also do mention from time-to-time more rigorous material on AI and encourage you all to dig into those deeper and more formal materials if so interested.

I am also an AI practitioner. This means that I write AI software for a living. Currently, I head-up the Cybernetics Self-Driving Car Institute, where we are developing AI software for self-driving cars.

For those of you that are reading this book and have a penchant for writing code, you might consider taking a look at the open source code available for self-driving cars. This is a handy place to start learning how to develop AI for self-driving cars. There are also many new educational courses spring forth. There is a growing body of those wanting to learn about and develop self-driving cars, and a growing body of colleges, labs, and other avenues by which you can learn about self-driving cars.

This book will provide a foundation of aspects that I think will get you ready for those kinds of more advanced training opportunities. If you've already taken those classes, you'll likely find these essays especially interesting as they offer a perspective that I am betting few other instructors or faculty offered to you. These are challenging essays that ask you to think beyond the conventional about self-driving cars.

THE MOTHER OF ALL AI PROJECTS

In June 2017, Apple CEO Tim Cook came out and finally admitted that Apple has been working on a self-driving car. As you'll see in my essays, Apple was enmeshed in secrecy about their self-driving car efforts. We have only been able to read the tea leaves and guess at what Apple has been up to. The notion of an iCar has been floating for quite a while, and self-driving engineers and researchers have been signing tight-lipped Non-Disclosure Agreements (NDA's) to work on projects at Apple that were as shrouded in mystery as any military invasion plans might be.

Tim Cook said something that many others in the Artificial Intelligence (AI) field have been saying, namely, the creation of a self-driving car has got to be the mother of all AI projects. In other words, it is in fact a tremendous moonshot for AI. If a self-driving car can be crafted and the AI works as we hope, it means that we have made incredible strides with AI and that therefore it opens many other worlds of potential breakthrough accomplishments that AI can solve.

Is this hyperbole? Am I just trying to make AI seem like a miracle worker and so provide self-aggrandizing statements for those of us writing the AI software for self-driving cars? No, it is not hyperbole. Developing a true self-driving car is really, really, really hard to do. Let me take a moment to explain why. As a side note, I realize that the Apple CEO is known for at times uttering hyperbole, and he had previously said for example that the year 2012 was "the mother of all years," and he had said that the release of iOS 10 was "the mother of all releases" – all of which does suggest he likes to use the handy "mother of" expression. But, I assure you, in terms of true self-driving cars, he has hit the nail on the head. For sure.

When you think about a moonshot and how we got to the moon, there are some identifiable characteristics and those same aspects can be applied to creating a true self-driving car. You'll notice that I keep putting the word "true" in front of the self-driving car expression. I do so because as per my essay about the various levels of self-driving cars, there are some self-driving cars that are only somewhat of a self-driving car. The somewhat versions are ones that require a human driver to be ready to intervene. In my view, that's not a true self-driving car. A true self-driving car is one that requires no human driver intervention at all. It is a car that can entirely undertake via automation the driving task without any human driver needed. This is the essence of what is known as a Level 5 self-driving car. We are currently at the Level 2 and Level 3 mark, and not yet at Level 5.

Getting to the moon involved aspects such as having big stretch goals, incremental progress, experimentation, innovation, and so on. Let's review how this applied to the moonshot of the bygone era, and how it applies to the self-driving car moonshot of today.

Big Stretch Goal

Trying to take a human and deliver the human to the moon, and bring them back, safely, was an extremely large stretch goal at the time. No one knew whether it could be done. The technology wasn't available yet. The cost was huge. The determination would need to be fierce. Etc. To reach a Level 5 self-driving car is going to be the same. It is a big stretch goal. We can readily get to the Level 3, and we are able to see the Level 4 just up ahead, but a Level 5 is still an unknown as to if it is doable. It should eventually be doable and in the same way that we thought we'd eventually get to the moon, but when it will occur is a different story.

Incremental Progress

Getting to the moon did not happen overnight in one fell swoop. It took years and years of incremental progress to get there. Likewise for self-driving cars. Google has famously been striving to get to the Level 5, and pretty much been willing to forgo dealing with the intervening levels, but most of the other self-driving car makers are doing the incremental route. Let's get a good Level 2 and a somewhat Level 3 going. Then, let's improve the Level 3 and get a somewhat Level 4 going. Then, let's improve the Level 4 and finally arrive at a Level 5. This seems to be the prevalent way that we are going to achieve the true self-driving car.

Experimentation

You likely know that there were various experiments involved in perfecting the approach and technology to get to the moon. As per making incremental progress, we first tried to see if we could get a rocket to go into space and safety return, then put a monkey in there, then with a human, then we went all the way to the moon but didn't land, and finally we arrived at the mission that actually landed on the moon.

Self-driving cars are the same way. We are doing simulations of self-driving cars. We do testing of self-driving cars on private land under controlled situations.

We do testing of self-driving cars on public roadways, often having to meet regulatory requirements including for example having an engineer or equivalent in the car to take over the controls if needed. And so on. Experiments big and small are needed to figure out what works and what doesn't.

Innovation

There are already some advances in AI that are allowing us to progress toward self-driving cars. We are going to need even more advances. Innovation in all aspects of technology are going to be required to achieve a true self-driving car. By no means do we already have everything in-hand that we need to get there. Expect new inventions and new approaches, new algorithms, etc.

Setbacks

Most of the pundits are avoiding talking about potential setbacks in the progress toward self-driving cars. Getting to the moon involved many setbacks, some of which you never have heard of and were buried at the time so as to not dampen enthusiasm and funding for getting to the moon. A recurring theme in many of my included essays is that there are going to be setbacks as we try to arrive at a true self-driving car. Take a deep breath and be ready. I just hope the setbacks don't completely stop progress. I am sure that it will cause progress to alter in a manner that we've not yet seen in the self-driving car field. I liken the self-driving car of today to the excitement everyone had for Uber when it first got going. Today, we have a different view of Uber and with each passing day there are more regulations to the ride sharing business and more concerns raised. The darling child only stays a darling until finally that child acts up. It will happen the same with self-driving cars.

SELF-DRIVING CARS CHALLENGES

But what exactly makes things so hard to have a true self-driving car, you might be asking. You have seen cruise control for years and years. You've lately seen cars that can do parallel parking. You've seen YouTube videos of Tesla drivers that put their hands out the window as their car zooms along the highway, and seen to therefore be in a self-driving car. Aren't we just needing to put a few more sensors onto a car and then we'll have in-hand a true self-driving car? Nope.

Consider for a moment the nature of the driving task. We don't just let anyone at any age drive a car. Worldwide, most countries won't license a driver until the age of 18, though many do allow a learner's permit at the age of 15 or 16. Some suggest that a younger age would be physically too small to reach the controls of the car. Though this might be the case, we could easily adjust the controls to allow for younger aged and thus smaller stature. It's not their physical size that matters. It's their cognitive development that matters.

To drive a car, you need to be able to reason about the car, what the car can and cannot do. You need to know how to operate the car. You need to know about how other cars on the road drive. You need to know what is allowed in driving such as speed limits and driving within marked lanes. You need to be able to react to situations and be able to avoid getting into accidents. You need to ascertain when to hit your brakes, when to steer clear of a pedestrian, and how to keep from ramming that motorcyclist that just cut you off.

Many of us had taken courses on driving. We studied about driving and took driver training. We had to take a test and pass it to be able to drive. The point being that though most adults take the driving task for granted, and we often "mindlessly" drive our cars, there is a significant amount of cognitive effort that goes into driving a car. After a while, it becomes second nature. You don't especially think about how you drive, you just do it. But, if you watch a novice driver, say a teenager learning to drive, you suddenly realize that there is a lot more complexity to it than we seem to realize.

Furthermore, driving is a very serious task. I recall when my daughter and son first learned to drive. They are both very conscientious people. They wanted to make sure that whatever they did, they did well, and that they did not harm anyone. Every day, when you get into a car, it is probably around 4,000 pounds of hefty metal and plastics (about two tons), and it is a lethal weapon. Think about it. You drive down the street in an object that weighs two tons and with the engine it can accelerate and ram into anything you want to hit. The damage a car can inflict is very scary. Both my children were surprised that they were being given the right to maneuver this monster of a beast that could cause tremendous harm entirely by merely letting go of the steering wheel for a moment or taking your eyes off the road.

In fact, in the United States alone there are about 30,000 deaths per year by auto accidents, which is around 100 per day. Given that there are about 263 million cars in the United States, I am actually more amazed that the number of fatalities is not a lot higher.

During my morning commute, I look at all the thousands of cars on the freeway around me, and I think that if all of them decided to go zombie and drive in a crazy maniac way, there would be many people dead. Somehow, incredibly, each day, most people drive relatively safely. To me, that's a miracle right there. Getting millions and millions of people to be safe and sane when behind the wheel of a two ton mobile object, it's a feat that we as a society should admire with pride.

So, hopefully you are in agreement that the driving task requires a great deal of cognition. You don't' need to be especially smart to drive a car, and we've done quite a bit to make car driving viable for even the average dolt. There isn't an IQ test that you need to take to drive a car. If you can read and write, and pass a test, you pretty much can legally drive a car. There are of course some that drive a car and are not legally permitted to do so, plus there are private areas such as farms where drivers are young, but for public roadways in the United States, you can be generally of average intelligence (or less) and be able to legally drive.

This though makes it seem like the cognitive effort must not be much. If the cognitive effort was truly hard, wouldn't we only have Einstein's that could drive a car? We have made sure to keep the driving task as simple as we can, by making the controls easy and relatively standardized, and by having roads that are relatively standardized, and so on. It is as though Disneyland has put their Autopia into the real-world, by us all as a society agreeing that roads will be a certain way, and we'll all abide by the various rules of driving.

A modest cognitive task by a human is still something that stymies AI. You certainly know that AI has been able to beat chess players and be good at other kinds of games. This type of narrow cognition is not what car driving is about. Car driving is much wider. It requires knowledge about the world, which a chess playing AI system does not need to know. The cognitive aspects of driving are on the one hand seemingly simple, but at the same time require layer upon layer of knowledge about cars, people, roads, rules, and a myriad of other "common sense" aspects. We don't have any AI systems today that have that same kind of breadth and depth of awareness and knowledge.

As revealed in my essays, the self-driving car of today is using trickery to do particular tasks. It is all very narrow in operation. Plus, it currently assumes that a human driver is ready to intervene. It is like a child that we have taught to stack blocks, but we are needed to be right there in case the child stacks them too high and they begin to fall over.

AI of today is brittle, it is narrow, and it does not approach the cognitive abilities of humans. This is why the true self-driving car is somewhere out in the future.

Another aspect to the driving task is that it is not solely a mind exercise. You do need to use your senses to drive. You use your eyes a vision sensors to see the road ahead. You vision capability is like a streaming video, which your brain needs to continually analyze as you drive. Where is the road? Is there a pedestrian in the way? Is there another car ahead of you? Your senses are relying a flood of info to your brain. Self-driving cars are trying to do the same, by using cameras, radar, ultrasound, and lasers. This is an attempt at mimicking how humans have senses and sensory apparatus.

Thus, the driving task is mental and physical. You use your senses, you use your arms and legs to manipulate the controls of the car, and you use your brain to assess the sensory info and direct your limbs to act upon the controls of the car. This all happens instantly. If you've ever perhaps gotten something in your eye and only had one eye available to drive with, you suddenly realize how dependent upon vision you are. If you have a broken foot with a cast, you suddenly realize how hard it is to control the brake pedal and the accelerator. If you've taken medication and your brain is maybe sluggish, you suddenly realize how much mental strain is required to drive a car.

An AI system that plays chess only needs to be focused on playing chess. The physical aspects aren't important because usually a human moves the chess pieces or the chessboard is shown on an electronic display. Using AI for a more life-and-death task such as analyzing MRI images of patients, this again does not require physical capabilities and instead is done by examining images of bits.

Driving a car is a true life-and-death task. It is a use of AI that can easily and at any moment produce death. For those colleagues of mine that are developing this AI, as am I, we need to keep in mind the somber aspects of this. We are producing software that will have in its virtual hands the lives of the occupants of the car, and the lives of those in other nearby cars, and the lives of nearby pedestrians, etc. Chess is not usually a life-or-death matter.

Driving is all around us. Cars are everywhere. Most of today's AI applications involve only a small number of people. Or, they are behind the scenes and we as humans have other recourse if the AI messes up. AI that is driving a car at 80 miles per hour on a highway had better not mess up. The consequences are grave.

Multiply this by the number of cars, if we could put magically self-driving into every car in the USA, we'd have AI running in the 263 million cars. That's a lot of AI spread around. This is AI on a massive scale that we are not doing today and that offers both promise and potential peril.

There are some that want AI for self-driving cars because they envision a world without any car accidents. They envision a world in which there is no car congestion and all cars cooperate with each other. These are wonderful utopian visions.

They are also very misleading. The adoption of self-driving cars is going to be incremental and not overnight. We cannot economically just junk all existing cars. Nor are we going to be able to affordably retrofit existing cars. It is more likely that self-driving cars will be built into new cars and that over many years of gradual replacement of existing cars that we'll see the mix of self-driving cars become substantial in the real-world.

In these essays, I have tried to offer technological insights without being overly technical in my description, and also blended the business, societal, and economic aspects too. Technologists need to consider the non-technological impacts of what they do. Non-technologists should be aware of what is being developed.

We all need to work together to collectively be prepared for the enormous disruption and transformative aspects of true self-driving cars.

WHAT THIS BOOK PROVIDES

What does this book provide to you? It introduces many of the key elements about self-driving cars and does so with an AI based perspective. I weave together technical and non-technical aspects, readily going from being concerned about the cognitive capabilities of the driving task and how the technology is embodying this into self-driving cars, and in the next breath I discuss the societal and economic aspects.

They are all intertwined because that's the way reality is. You cannot separate out the technology per se, and instead must consider it within the milieu of what is being invented and innovated, and do so with a mindset towards the contemporary mores and culture that shape what we are doing and what we hope to do.

WHY THIS BOOK

I wrote this book to try and bring to the public view many aspects about self-driving cars that nobody seems to be discussing.

For business leaders that are either involved in making self-driving cars or that are going to leverage self-driving cars, I hope that this book will enlighten you as to the risks involved and ways in which you should be strategizing about how to deal with those risks.

For entrepreneurs, startups and other businesses that want to enter into the self-driving car market that is emerging, I hope this book sparks your interest in doing so, and provides some sense of what might be prudent to pursue.

For researchers that study self-driving cars, I hope this book spurs your interest in the risks and safety issues of self-driving cars, and also nudges you toward conducting research on those aspects.

For students in computer science or related disciplines, I hope this book will provide you with interesting and new ideas and material, for which you might conduct research or provide some career direction insights for you.

For AI companies and high-tech companies pursuing self-driving cars, this book will hopefully broaden your view beyond just the mere coding and development needed to make self-driving cars.

For all readers, I hope that you will find the material in this book to be stimulating. Some of it will be repetitive of things you already know. But I am pretty sure that you'll also find various eureka moments whereby you'll discover a new technique or approach that you had not earlier thought of. I am also betting that there will be material that forces you to rethink some of your current practices.

I am not saying you will suddenly have an epiphany and change what you are doing. I do think though that you will reconsider or perhaps revisit what you are doing.

For anyone choosing to use this book for teaching purposes, please take a look at my suggestions for doing so, as described in the Appendix. I have found the material handy in courses that I have taught, and likewise other faculty have told me that they have found the material handy, in some cases as extended readings and in other instances as a core part of their course (depending on the nature of the class).

In my writing for this book, I have tried carefully to blend both the practitioner and the academic styles of writing.

It is not as abstract as is typical academic journal writing, but at the same time offers depth by going into the nuances and trade-offs of various practices.

The word "deep" is in vogue today, meaning getting deeply into a subject or topic, and so is the word "unpack" which means to tease out the underlying aspects of a subject or topic. I have sought to offer material that addresses an issue or topic by going relatively deeply into it and make sure that it is well unpacked.

In any book about AI, it is difficult to use our everyday words without having some of them be misinterpreted. Specifically, it is easy to anthropomorphize AI. When I say that an AI system "knows" something, I do not want you to construe that the AI system has sentience and "knows" in the same way that humans do. They aren't that way, as yet. I have tried to use quotes around such words from time-to-time to emphasize that the words I am using should not be misinterpreted to ascribe true human intelligence to the AI systems that we know of today. If I used quotes around all such words, the book would be very difficult to read, and so I am doing so judiciously. Please keep that in mind as you read the material, thanks.

Some of the material is time-based in terms of covering underway activities, and though some of it might decay, nonetheless I believe you'll find the material useful and informative.

COMPANION BOOKS BY DR. ELIOT

1. **"Introduction to Driverless Self-Driving Cars"** by Dr. Lance Eliot
2. **"Innovation and Thought Leadership on Self-Driving Driverless Cars"**
3. **"Advances in AI and Autonomous Vehicles: Cybernetic Self-Driving Cars"**
4. **"Self-Driving Cars: The Mother of All AI Projects"** by Dr. Lance Eliot
5. **"New Advances in AI Autonomous Driverless Self-Driving Cars"**
6. **"Autonomous Vehicle Driverless Self-Driving Cars and Artificial Intelligence"** by Dr. Lance Eliot and Michael B. Eliot
7. **"Transformative Artificial Intelligence Driverless Self-Driving Cars"**
8. **"Disruptive Artificial Intelligence and Driverless Self-Driving Cars"**
9. "State-of-the-Art AI Driverless Self-Driving Cars" by Dr. Lance Eliot
10. "Top Trends in AI Self-Driving Cars" by Dr. Lance Eliot
11. **"AI Innovations and Self-Driving Cars"** by Dr. Lance Eliot
12. **"Crucial Advances for AI Driverless Cars"** by Dr. Lance Eliot
13. **"Sociotechnical Insights and AI Driverless Cars"** by Dr. Lance Eliot.
14. **"Pioneering Advances for AI Driverless Cars"** by Dr. Lance Eliot
15. **"Leading Edge Trends for AI Driverless Cars"** by Dr. Lance Eliot
16. **"The Cutting Edge of AI Autonomous Cars"** by Dr. Lance Eliot
17. **"The Next Wave of AI Self-Driving Cars"** by Dr. Lance Eliot
18. **"Revolutionary Innovations of AI Driverless Cars"** by Dr. Lance Eliot
19. **"AI Self-Driving Cars Breakthroughs"** by Dr. Lance Eliot
20. **"Trailblazing Trends for AI Self-Driving Cars"** by Dr. Lance Eliot
21. **"Ingenious Strides for AI Driverless Cars"** by Dr. Lance Eliot
22. **"AI Self-Driving Cars Inventiveness"** by Dr. Lance Eliot
23. **"Visionary Secrets of AI Driverless Cars"** by Dr. Lance Eliot
24. **"Spearheading AI Self-Driving Cars"** by Dr. Lance Eliot
25. **"Spurring AI Self-Driving Cars"** by Dr. Lance Eliot
26. **"Avant-Garde AI Driverless Cars"** by Dr. Lance Eliot
27. **"AI Self-Driving Cars Evolvement"** by Dr. Lance Eliot
28. **"AI Driverless Cars Chrysalis"** by Dr. Lance Eliot
29. **"Boosting AI Autonomous Cars"** by Dr. Lance Eliot
30. **"AI Self-Driving Cars Trendsetting"** by Dr. Lance Eliot
31. **"AI Autonomous Cars Forefront"** by Dr. Lance Eliot
32. **"AI Autonomous Cars Emergence"** by Dr. Lance Eliot
33. **"AI Autonomous Cars Progress"** by Dr. Lance Eliot
34. **"AI Self-Driving Cars Prognosis"** by Dr. Lance Eliot
35. **"AI Self-Driving Cars Momentum"** by Dr. Lance Eliot
36. **"AI Self-Driving Cars Headway"** by Dr. Lance Eliot
37. **"AI Self-Driving Cars Vicissitude"** by Dr. Lance Eliot
38. **"AI Self-Driving Cars Autonomy"** by Dr. Lance Eliot
39. **"AI Driverless Cars Transmutation"** by Dr. Lance Eliot
40. **"AI Driverless Cars Potentiality"** by Dr. Lance Eliot
41. **"AI Driverless Cars Realities"** by Dr. Lance Eliot
42. **"AI Self-Driving Cars Materiality"** by Dr. Lance Eliot
43. **"AI Self-Driving Cars Accordance"** by Dr. Lance Eliot

These books are available on Amazon and at other major global booksellers.

Dr. Lance B. Eliot

CHAPTER 1

ELIOT FRAMEWORK FOR AI SELF-DRIVING CARS

CHAPTER 1

ELIOT FRAMEWORK FOR AI SELF-DRIVING CARS

This chapter is a core foundational aspect for understanding AI self-driving cars and I have used this same chapter in several of my other books to introduce the reader to essential elements of this field. Once you've read this chapter, you'll be prepared to read the rest of the material since the foundational essence of the components of autonomous AI driverless self-driving cars will have been established for you.

––––––––

When I give presentations about self-driving cars and teach classes on the topic, I have found it helpful to provide a framework around which the various key elements of self-driving cars can be understood and organized (see diagram at the end of this chapter). The framework needs to be simple enough to convey the overarching elements, but at the same time not so simple that it belies the true complexity of self-driving cars. As such, I am going to describe the framework here and try to offer in a thousand words (or more!) what the framework diagram itself intends to portray.

The core elements on the diagram are numbered for ease of reference. The numbering does not suggest any kind of prioritization of the elements. Each element is crucial. Each element has a purpose, and otherwise would not be included in the framework. For some self-driving cars, a particular element might be more important or somehow distinguished in comparison to other self-driving cars.

You could even use the framework to rate a particular self-driving car, doing so by gauging how well it performs in each of the elements of the framework. I will describe each of the elements, one at a time. After doing so, I'll discuss aspects that illustrate how the elements interact and perform during the overall effort of a self-driving car.

At the AI Self-Driving Car Institute, we use the framework to keep track of what we are working on, and how we are developing software that fills in what is needed to achieve Level 5 self-driving cars.

D-01: Sensor Capture

Let's start with the one element that often gets the most attention in the press about self-driving cars, namely, the sensory devices for a self-driving car.

On the framework, the box labeled as D-01 indicates "Sensor Capture" and refers to the processes of the self-driving car that involve collecting data from the myriad of sensors that are used for a self-driving car. The types of devices typically involved are listed, such as the use of mono cameras, stereo cameras, LIDAR devices, radar systems, ultrasonic devices, GPS, IMU, and so on.

These devices are tasked with obtaining data about the status of the self-driving car and the world around it. Some of the devices are continually providing updates, while others of the devices await an indication by the self-driving car that the device is supposed to collect data. The data might be first transformed in some fashion by the device itself, or it might instead be fed directly into the sensor capture as raw data. At that point, it might be up to the sensor capture processes to do transformations on the data. This all varies depending upon the nature of the devices being used and how the devices were designed and developed.

D-02: Sensor Fusion

Imagine that your eyeballs receive visual images, your nose receives odors, your ears receive sounds, and in essence each of your distinct sensory devices is getting some form of input. The input befits the nature of the device. Likewise, for a self-driving car, the cameras provide visual images, the radar returns radar reflections, and so on. Each device provides the data as befits what the device does.

At some point, using the analogy to humans, you need to merge together what your eyes see, what your nose smells, what your ears hear, and piece it all together into a larger sense of what the world is all about and what is happening around you. Sensor fusion is the action of taking the singular aspects from each of the devices and putting them together into a larger puzzle.

Sensor fusion is a tough task. There are some devices that might not be working at the time of the sensor capture. Or, there might some devices that are unable to report well what they have detected. Again, using a human analogy, suppose you are in a dark room and so your eyes cannot see much. At that point, you might need to rely more so on your ears and what you hear. The same is true for a self-driving car. If the cameras are obscured due to snow and sleet, it might be that the radar can provide a greater indication of what the external conditions consist of.

In the case of a self-driving car, there can be a plethora of such sensory devices. Each is reporting what it can. Each might have its difficulties. Each might have its limitations, such as how far ahead it can detect an object. All of these limitations need to be considered during the sensor fusion task.

D-03: Virtual World Model

For humans, we presumably keep in our minds a model of the world around us when we are driving a car. In your mind, you know that the car is going at say 60 miles per hour and that you are on a freeway.

You have a model in your mind that your car is surrounded by other cars, and that there are lanes to the freeway. Your model is not only based on what you can see, hear, etc., but also what you know about the nature of the world. You know that at any moment that car ahead of you can smash on its brakes, or the car behind you can ram into your car, or that the truck in the next lane might swerve into your lane.

The AI of the self-driving car needs to have a virtual world model, which it then keeps updated with whatever it is receiving from the sensor fusion, which received its input from the sensor capture and the sensory devices.

D-04: System Action Plan

By having a virtual world model, the AI of the self-driving car is able to keep track of where the car is and what is happening around the car. In addition, the AI needs to determine what to do next. Should the self-driving car hit its brakes? Should the self-driving car stay in its lane or swerve into the lane to the left? Should the self-driving car accelerate or slow down?

A system action plan needs to be prepared by the AI of the self-driving car. The action plan specifies what actions should be taken. The actions need to pertain to the status of the virtual world model. Plus, the actions need to be realizable.

This realizability means that the AI cannot just assert that the self-driving car should suddenly sprout wings and fly. Instead, the AI must be bound by whatever the self-driving car can actually do, such as coming to a halt in a distance of X feet at a speed of Y miles per hour, rather than perhaps asserting that the self-driving car come to a halt in 0 feet as though it could instantaneously come to a stop while it is in motion.

D-05: Controls Activation

The system action plan is implemented by activating the controls of the car to act according to what the plan stipulates.

This might mean that the accelerator control is commanded to increase the speed of the car. Or, the steering control is commanded to turn the steering wheel 30 degrees to the left or right.

One question arises as to whether or not the controls respond as they are commanded to do. In other words, suppose the AI has commanded the accelerator to increase, but for some reason it does not do so. Or, maybe it tries to do so, but the speed of the car does not increase. The controls activation feeds back into the virtual world model, and simultaneously the virtual world model is getting updated from the sensors, the sensor capture, and the sensor fusion. This allows the AI to ascertain what has taken place as a result of the controls being commanded to take some kind of action.

By the way, please keep in mind that though the diagram seems to have a linear progression to it, the reality is that these are all aspects of the self-driving car that are happening in parallel and simultaneously. The sensors are capturing data, meanwhile the sensor fusion is taking place, meanwhile the virtual model is being updated, meanwhile the system action plan is being formulated and reformulated, meanwhile the controls are being activated.

This is the same as a human being that is driving a car. They are eyeballing the road, meanwhile they are fusing in their mind the sights, sounds, etc., meanwhile their mind is updating their model of the world around them, meanwhile they are formulating an action plan of what to do, and meanwhile they are pushing their foot onto the pedals and steering the car. In the normal course of driving a car, you are doing all of these at once. I mention this so that when you look at the diagram, you will think of the boxes as processes that are all happening at the same time, and not as though only one happens and then the next.

They are shown diagrammatically in a simplistic manner to help comprehend what is taking place. You though should also realize that they are working in parallel and simultaneous with each other. This is a tough aspect in that the inter-element communications involve latency and other aspects that must be taken into account.

There can be delays in one element updating and then sharing its latest status with other elements.

D-06: Automobile & CAN

Contemporary cars use various automotive electronics and a Controller Area Network (CAN) to serve as the components that underlie the driving aspects of a car. There are Electronic Control Units (ECU's) which control subsystems of the car, such as the engine, the brakes, the doors, the windows, and so on.

The elements D-01, D-02, D-03, D-04, D-05 are layered on top of the D-06, and must be aware of the nature of what the D-06 is able to do and not do.

D-07: In-Car Commands

Humans are going to be occupants in self-driving cars. In a Level 5 self-driving car, there must be some form of communication that takes place between the humans and the self-driving car. For example, I go into a self-driving car and tell it that I want to be driven over to Disneyland, and along the way I want to stop at In-and-Out Burger. The self-driving car now parses what I've said and tries to then establish a means to carry out my wishes.

In-car commands can happen at any time during a driving journey. Though my example was about an in-car command when I first got into my self-driving car, it could be that while the self-driving car is carrying out the journey that I change my mind. Perhaps after getting stuck in traffic, I tell the self-driving car to forget about getting the burgers and just head straight over to the theme park. The self-driving car needs to be alert to in-car commands throughout the journey.

D-08: V2X Communications

We will ultimately have self-driving cars communicating with each other, doing so via V2V (Vehicle-to-Vehicle) communications.

We will also have self-driving cars that communicate with the roadways and other aspects of the transportation infrastructure, doing so via V2I (Vehicle-to-Infrastructure).

The variety of ways in which a self-driving car will be communicating with other cars and infrastructure is being called V2X, whereby the letter X means whatever else we identify as something that a car should or would want to communicate with. The V2X communications will be taking place simultaneous with everything else on the diagram, and those other elements will need to incorporate whatever it gleans from those V2X communications.

D-09: Deep Learning

The use of Deep Learning permeates all other aspects of the self-driving car. The AI of the self-driving car will be using deep learning to do a better job at the systems action plan, and at the control's activation, and at the sensor fusion, and so on.

Currently, the use of artificial neural networks is the most prevalent form of deep learning. Based on large swaths of data, the neural networks attempt to "learn" from the data and therefore direct the efforts of the self-driving car accordingly.

D-10: Tactical AI

Tactical AI is the element of dealing with the moment-to-moment driving of the self-driving car. Is the self-driving car staying in its lane of the freeway? Is the car responding appropriately to the controls commands? Are the sensory devices working?

For human drivers, the tactical equivalent can be seen when you watch a novice driver such as a teenager that is first driving. They are focused on the mechanics of the driving task, keeping their eye on the road while also trying to properly control the car.

D-11: Strategic AI

The Strategic AI aspects of a self-driving car are dealing with the larger picture of what the self-driving car is trying to do. If I had asked that the self-driving car take me to Disneyland, there is an overall journey map that needs to be kept and maintained.

There is an interaction between the Strategic AI and the Tactical AI. The Strategic AI is wanting to keep on the mission of the driving, while the Tactical AI is focused on the particulars underway in the driving effort. If the Tactical AI seems to wander away from the overarching mission, the Strategic AI wants to see why and get things back on track. If the Tactical AI realizes that there is something amiss on the self-driving car, it needs to alert the Strategic AI accordingly and have an adjustment to the overarching mission that is underway.

D-12: Self-Aware AI

Very few of the self-driving cars being developed are including a Self-Aware AI element, which we at the Cybernetic Self-Driving Car Institute believe is crucial to Level 5 self-driving cars.

The Self-Aware AI element is intended to watch over itself, in the sense that the AI is making sure that the AI is working as intended. Suppose you had a human driving a car, and they were starting to drive erratically. Hopefully, their own self-awareness would make them realize they themselves are driving poorly, such as perhaps starting to fall asleep after having been driving for hours on end. If you had a passenger in the car, they might be able to alert the driver if the driver is starting to do something amiss.

This is exactly what the Self-Aware AI element tries to do, it becomes the overseer of the AI, and tries to detect when the AI has become faulty or confused, and then find ways to overcome the issue.

D-13: Economic

The economic aspects of a self-driving car are not per se a technology aspect of a self-driving car, but the economics do indeed impact the nature of a self-driving car. For example, the cost of outfitting a self-driving car with every kind of possible sensory device is prohibitive, and so choices need to be made about which devices are used. And, for those sensory devices chosen, whether they would have a full set of features or a more limited set of features.

We are going to have self-driving cars that are at the low-end of a consumer cost point, and others at the high-end of a consumer cost point. You cannot expect that the self-driving car at the low-end is going to be as robust as the one at the high-end. I realize that many of the self-driving car pundits are acting as though all self-driving cars will be the same, but they won't be. Just like anything else, we are going to have self-driving cars that have a range of capabilities. Some will be better than others. Some will be safer than others. This is the way of the real-world, and so we need to be thinking about the economics aspects when considering the nature of self-driving cars.

D-14: Societal

This component encompasses the societal aspects of AI which also impacts the technology of self-driving cars. For example, the famous Trolley Problem involves what choices should a self-driving car make when faced with life-and-death matters. If the self-driving car is about to either hit a child standing in the roadway, or instead ram into a tree at the side of the road and possibly kill the humans in the self-driving car, which choice should be made?

We need to keep in mind the societal aspects will underlie the AI of the self-driving car. Whether we are aware of it explicitly or not, the AI will have embedded into it various societal assumptions.

D-15: Innovation

I included the notion of innovation into the framework because we can anticipate that whatever a self-driving car consists of, it will continue to be innovated over time. The self-driving cars coming out in the next several years will undoubtedly be different and less innovative than the versions that come out in ten years hence, and so on.

Framework Overall

For those of you that want to learn about self-driving cars, you can potentially pick a particular element and become specialized in that aspect. Some engineers are focusing on the sensory devices. Some engineers focus on the controls activation. And so on. There are specialties in each of the elements.

Researchers are likewise specializing in various aspects. For example, there are researchers that are using Deep Learning to see how best it can be used for sensor fusion. There are other researchers that are using Deep Learning to derive good System Action Plans. Some are studying how to develop AI for the Strategic aspects of the driving task, while others are focused on the Tactical aspects.

A well-prepared all-around software developer that is involved in self-driving cars should be familiar with all of the elements, at least to the degree that they know what each element does. This is important since whatever piece of the pie that the software developer works on, they need to be knowledgeable about what the other elements are doing.

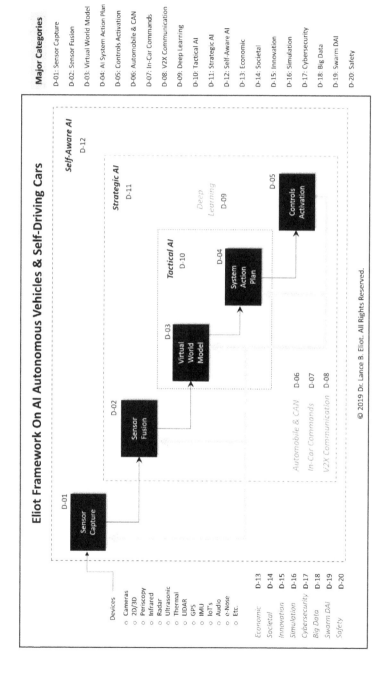

Eliot Framework On AI Autonomous Vehicles & Self-Driving Cars

© 2019 Dr. Lance B. Eliot. All Rights Reserved.

CHAPTER 2
REGULATORY SCAPEGOATING AND AI SELF-DRIVING CARS

CHAPTER 2

REGULATORY SCAPEGOATING AND AI SELF-DRIVING CARS

A tweet by Elon Musk during the Easter 2020 weekend has sprung forth an erstwhile Easter egg hunt by the media and industry about the self-driving car status of Tesla.

Let's first consider the self-driving car ambitions of Tesla and then get to Musk's latest tweet.

Turn back the clock by about seven months or so.

During a Tesla earnings call in October of last year (that's 2019), Elon Musk had indicated this about the Tesla-coined FSD (Full Self-Driving) status: "While it's going to be tight, it still does appear that will be at least in limited early access release of a feature complete self-driving feature this year" (the reference to "this year" meant the year 2019, since the comment was made in 2019).

That hedged promise did not seem to come to fruition in 2019.

There is also the ongoing lack of clarification about what a "feature complete" kind of self-driving portends since there is no clear-cut definition of this rather vague and made-up phrase (it isn't any recognizable vernacular or industry parlance, certainly not codified by self-driving car industry standards, so essentially a nebulous Musk-phraseology non-specified enigma).

The only shard of a clue might be that Musk also suggested the Tesla's might be "able to be autonomous but requiring supervision and intervention at times," as part of the feature complete notion.

As a background about self-driving, it is important to realize that of the officially defined levels of autonomy per the SAE (Society of Automotive Engineers) standard, if a self-driving car needs a human driver, the self-driving car is said to be semi-autonomous and not fully autonomous.

Since Musk was indicating that a Tesla embodying a "feature complete" self-driving capability would also require that a human driver supervise and be ready to intervene, it would be best to say that the Tesla's would be semi-autonomous so as to not conflate with the type of self-driving car that is truly autonomous.

That's why using just the word "autonomous" by itself is not a good way to express things, since it then creates ambiguity around whether the vehicle will be either semi-autonomous or fully autonomous.

Furthermore, in some respects, using just the word autonomous by itself can mislead by implying that a car is intending to be fully autonomous (meaning that a human driver is not needed, at all, for any reason), given that most people would infer that the word "autonomous" in of itself carries the notion of being wholly autonomous.

It might seem like splitting hairs to be grinding one's teeth about the autonomous usage, but the wording does foretell a huge difference in what occurs.

What would be clearer for all parties would be for Musk and Tesla to simply adopt the use of the levels of autonomy as defined by the SAE official standard, which I'll explain in a moment.

As an aside, please know that there are some critics of the SAE standard that assert it ought to be replaced with an even more definitive set of levels, yet, despite that desire to be more stringent, nonetheless, the existing standard does provide a handy means of generally agreeing to what constitutes (for now) a measurable set of levels of autonomy. Thus, anyone that might try to use that criticism to entirely escape from referring to those existing levels is playing a kind of game, as it were, using the critics of the standard as a type of false protective shield to wave their hands in the air.

Some contend that the ambiguous wording by Musk and Tesla about the intended capabilities of the FSD is not somehow accidental and nor incidental. Rather, the belief is that the wording is purposeful and intentionally aiming to be hazy, allowing the firm to not be pinned down on any specifics.

In a sense, it might be likened to political speech that embraces broad platitudes and avoids any brass tacks, providing maximal flexibility and what some would refer to as the wink-wink form of plausible deniability.

In any case, subsequent to the statement by Musk on that earnings call, he later indicated that rather than the earlier prediction of things happening by the end of 2019 (which, yes, was hedged by his having said "it does still appear" in his initial claim), instead, the new target would be sometime in 2020.

Supporters would likely say that he's being forthright and candid and that it is obviously difficult to predict when this extremely complex software can be readied, especially for something as life-or-death and monumental as being able to aid in driving a car.

Others might counter with the point that this is a shell game of moving around the peanut to distract, and maybe there isn't any peanut sitting under the shells, or that the real date is perhaps in 2021 or 2022, but to pacify and keep people eagerly engaged that the drip-drip of make a date and then move the date is being teased.

Latest Musings By Musk On Tesla FSD

Fast forward to the Easter weekend of April 2020.

In response to a tweeted question about the latest status of FSD for Tesla's, Musk responded with this tweet: "Functionality still looking good for this year. Regulatory approval is the big unknown."

For those that read the tea leaves, once again there is a hedge in the "looking good" portion of his remark.

Looking good could mean that things will happen by "this year" or could be interpreted to suggest that at this moment things are seemingly on-track, but that he's implying there's some chance it might not proceed apace, and therefore at a later time this year it will be readily possible to say that things took a bit of a turn and the date gets pushed further out, becoming perhaps an indefinite 2021 date.

There is also again the ambiguity about what will even be delivered per se since the word "functionality" has little definitive meaning and takes things back into the morass of what the feature complete and FSD actually consist of.

Presumably, it might be possible to showcase something that will be labeled as "functionality" within this year, hitting thusly the suggested promise, and yet the functionality might be a far cry from and a lot less than what seems to otherwise be implied as self-driving capabilities.

It's a wording that has lots of handy room for ambiguity and loose interpretation.

Supporters would likely applaud his willingness to share the latest status and emphasize that there's only so much one can say in a short tweet. Don't get so finicky and peck apart the wording, they might insist.

Many in the media certainly seemed to look past these semantic hedges and proclaimed that Musk indicated that the Tesla fleet of self-driving cars could be ready by the end of this year.

Coulda, woulda, shoulda, some critics say.

In any case, there is a subtle aspect to the tweet that few are perhaps giving its due.

Like driving on a lengthy stretch of open highway and seeing a distant object that's not quite yet in focus, the tweet contains a reference to regulatory approval, doing so as almost an aside.

As part of the ongoing rendition about Tesla and Musk, be aware that there have been many occasions whereby the firm and its CEO have made various remarks about potential regulatory aspects, including the notion that regulations are likely to impinge on the self-driving ambitions of Tesla (and, in theory, the rest of the self-driving car industry too).

Maybe it's time to more closely tackle that distant thing called regulatory approval, as it pertains particularly to Tesla, and see if via the use of a telescope we can bring the topic closer into focus.

Before doing so, let's take a moment to clarify the levels of self-driving cars and their autonomy.

The Levels Of Self-Driving Cars

True self-driving cars are ones that the AI drives the car entirely on its own and there isn't any human assistance during the driving task.

These driverless vehicles are considered a Level 4 and Level 5, while a car that requires a human driver to co-share the driving effort is usually considered at a Level 2 or Level 3. The cars that co-share the driving task are described as being semi-autonomous, and typically contain a variety of automated add-on's that are referred to as ADAS (Advanced Driver-Assistance Systems).

There is not yet a true self-driving car at Level 5, which we don't yet even know if this will be possible to achieve, and nor how long it will take to get there.

Meanwhile, the Level 4 efforts are gradually trying to get some traction by undergoing very narrow and selective public roadway trials, though there is controversy over whether this testing should be allowed per se (we are all life-or-death guinea pigs in an experiment taking place on our highways and byways, some point out).

Since semi-autonomous cars require a human driver, the adoption of those types of cars won't be markedly different than driving conventional vehicles, so there's not much new per se to cover about them on this topic (though, as you'll see in a moment, the points next made are generally applicable).

For semi-autonomous cars, it is important that the public needs to be forewarned about a disturbing aspect that's been arising lately, namely that in spite of those human drivers that keep posting videos of themselves falling asleep at the wheel of a Level 2 or Level 3 car, we all need to avoid being misled into believing that the driver can take away their attention from the driving task while driving a semi-autonomous car.

You are the responsible party for the driving actions of the vehicle, regardless of how much automation might be tossed into a Level 2 or Level 3.

Self-Driving Cars And Musk On Regulatory Approvals

For Level 4 and Level 5 true self-driving vehicles, there won't be a human driver involved in the driving task.

All occupants will be passengers.

The AI is doing the driving.

Existing Tesla's are not Level 4 and nor are they Level 5.

Most would classify them as Level 2 today.

What difference does that make?

Well, if you have a true self-driving car (Level 4 and Level 5), one that is being driven solely by the AI, there is no need for a human driver and indeed no interaction between the AI and a human driver.

For a Level 2 car, the human driver is still in the driver's seat.

Furthermore, the human driver is considered the responsible party for driving that car.

The twist that's going to mess everyone up is that the AI might seem to be able to drive the Level 2 car, meanwhile, it cannot, and thus the human driver still must be attentive and act as though they are driving the car.

With that as a crucial backdrop, given the haziness of whatever it is that Tesla is going to deliver if a human driver is still needed, this means that the "self-driving" is going to either be an enhanced version of Level 2 or maybe be a Level 3.

But, definitely not a Level 4 and nor a Level 5, assuming that the Tesla capability will require the presence of a human driver at the wheel.

Anyway, shift attention to the other element of this discussion, the aspect of regulatory approval.

Revisit the recent tweet of Musk, which said this: "Functionality still looking good for this year. Regulatory approval is the big unknown."

Given that the tweet was sent out during the Easter weekend, we should presumably be ready to go down the rabbit hole to pursue its meaning.

Here's what some contend.

We all generally perceive the government and regulations as a hurdle to progress and innovation (I'm not saying that's necessarily true, only that it is commonly perceived as such).

This somewhat anti-regulatory viewpoint is especially exhibited or at least touted by a maverick company like Tesla and a maverick person like Musk, and seemingly equally embraced by the maverick-like supporters that relish this passionate maverick-flavor thereof.

Could the use of a regulatory boogieman be a clever underlying element of a strategy that figures if the technical stuff continues to be arduous to get completed, it will be "easy" to switch over to the pretense that regulations are the source of the delays and not the actual technical roadblocks instead?

In essence, put out there a scapegoat, one not yet invoked, yet sitting at the ready, and when or if the time is rife, stoke it into the world sphere for all its worth.

Admittedly, this does have some sense to it.

How can an entity or person keep pushing out dates of delivery, and do so without ultimately getting harshly dinged for the continuing series of delays?

Well, that's easy, just blame the matter on those bureaucratic paper-pushers.

The beauty of such an excuse is that it seems to ring true in many ways, namely that the public already has a predisposition that regulations are oftentimes stifling and that it seems that many "new" innovations have only arisen via the flouting of existing laws and regulations (for example, some would argue vehemently that Uber and Lyft did just that, skirting the existent rules that everyday taxi and cab services have had to endure).

So, by putting into your back-pocket the regulatory signpost and peddling it quietly from time-to-time, the stage is being set to invoke the boogieman, when needed, if needed.

If that day arrives, you can pull the ripcord, blossoming the regulatory outrage parachute, along with triggering rabid fans to bellow "down with the man," buying needed breathing space and creating a saving grace smokescreen while hiding behind the stirred up outrage.

Of course, it might be that the scapegoat isn't otherwise needed and so it might never be invoked.

Or, the scapegoat might be needed, and just like a "Break Glass" fire alarm, at the right time and right place, the regulatory shaming can begin.

There is the other side of that coin too.

It might genuinely be the case that regulatory aspects might trip things up, in which case, the whole subtle theme is still a worthy undercurrent to keep warm and ready for use.

Here's part of the rub on that.

- **What is it that Tesla and Musk specifically believe will be a regulatory barrier or hurdle for their FSD or feature complete or whatever "it is" capabilities?**

There doesn't seem to be any specifics yet stated.

- **If they are able to foresee that there are regulatory issues, what are they doing right now to anticipate those facets?**

In other words, it doesn't seem businesswise prudent that if you knew of regulatory qualms that you wouldn't be readying for them, either by preparing your tech to cope accordingly or somehow be designed to achieve the regulatory requirements or by working hand-in-hand with the regulators to see if there are ways to adjust or amend those claimed concerns.

- **Why not layout directly for all to see what those gaps are between what the regulations require and what the anticipated tech will deliver?**

Seems like it would be pragmatic and an expedient way to head-off a pending difficulty or delay by being overt and proactive, rather than perhaps waiting until things are "readied" and then suddenly proclaiming, oops, can't go ahead due to a regulatory mandate.

Indeed, here's what Musk said in July of 2017: "AI is a rare case where we need to be proactive about regulation instead of reactive. Because I think by the time we are reactive in AI regulation, it's too late."

Sure, that does make a lot of sense.

This also raises the specter that regulations seem to nearly always get tainted as bad, but it would appear that Musk is actually noting that regulations might very well be warranted, at least with regard to AI-based systems (which would include self-driving cars, by the way).

Perhaps there is a sound basis for needed regulatory approval that Musk's recent tweet suggests will either be a complication or worse implies will be an impediment as an undue burden.

This brings us further to Musk's own words on the topic of needing AI-related regulations. In a tweet on February 17, 2020, Musk indicated this: "All orgs developing advanced AI should be regulated, including Tesla."

If that tweet is taken at face value, it would seem that rather than possibly being concerned about regulatory approval for the Tesla capabilities, instead, it is essentially on the wish list of something that needs to be done and rightfully should be done.

Now, you can certainly still argue about whether the regulations themselves are on-target or not, but this is an argument that ought to already be taking place and especially in a public manner, due to the life-or-death matters involving self-driving cars, both semi-autonomous and fully autonomous.

There are numerous efforts underway right now about the regulatory aspects associated with self-driving cars, including at the federal level, the states, the municipalities, and also abundant industry bodies that are furthering standards that will inevitably be wrapped into some form of regulations.

That being the case, what beef does Tesla or Musk have, which would be handy to know now, and be able to therefore either seek a shaping or reshaping of those efforts.

Is it something technical?

Or, it is that they believe it will take too much time to undertake, in which case, perhaps propose how the process ought to be streamlined, and yet hopefully still retain the needed safety and care expected by the public.

Conclusion

Supporters of Tesla and Musk would likely argue that the regulatory approval aspects are something that ought to not get in the way of achieving Tesla's self-driving ambitions.

Okay, if that's the case, it would seem helpful if a fully delineated list of either unnecessary regulations were identified, or if the regulations were perhaps overly bloated or superfluous and thus going to block or impede progress, explain what that is.

In July of 2017, Musk said this: "I have exposure to the very cutting-edge AI, and I think people should be really concerned about it."

Furthermore, his remarks of July 2017 included this: "I keep sounding the alarm bell, but until people see robots going down the street killing people, they don't know how to react, because it seems so ethereal."

Parlaying off his stated qualms, there some outspoken critics that worry we are heading toward self-driving cars that are going to be going down the streets and highways, potentially getting into car crashes, killing people, and thus the eerie predictive nature of Musk's own words are a foretelling of such potential.

It could be that well-crafted regulations and the enforcement of those regulations could aid in allying or to some degree mitigating Musk's rightfully sounded alarm bell, but you can't in the same breath be alluding to regulations as a seeming party crusher that is going to undermine matters, at least not if you aren't stating directly how that seems to be the case and taking proactive action accordingly.

I'm not making an argument per se here about the nature or need of regulations (that's an ongoing debate overall), and merely pointing out that regulations are a consideration for self-driving cars, for society, for our well-being, etc.

In the case of AI, some believe that we haven't sufficiently adjusted existing laws to enable the advances that AI is bringing to our everyday existence, while others are at times claiming that existing laws are going to stifle the adoption of AI.

Whichever camp you fall into, time to get into the game and start participating in the AI and laws discussions, doing so now, and aid in guiding the future of AI in our society.

CHAPTER 3
TRUST BELIEFS
AND
AI SELF-DRIVING CARS

CHAPTER 3

TRUST BELIEFS
AND
AI SELF-DRIVING CARS

Do you trust your fellow citizens?

Maybe, maybe not.

Or, more likely, you trust them to some degree, and therefore you somewhat trust them and somewhat do not trust them, assuming that trust exists on a spectrum ranging from full trust to little or no trust.

The trust that you exhibit might vary too as contingent upon contextual and situational differences.

Notably, the role of trust has become perceptible during the COVID-19 pandemic, providing a rather unique and adverse situational moment in our collective lives and one that is tugging harshly on our collective sense of trust.

How so?

Consider these facets.

When you go outside for a stroll, and if you are in an area observing social distancing, do you trust your fellow humans to abide by the six feet distance rule?

In some locales, those venturing outdoors appear to stringently obey the six-foot guideline and will freely step off a sidewalk into the street to ensure that the footage gap is preserved when encountering someone walking toward them on a sidewalk that only has a four-foot width.

Meanwhile, in other locales, people might be less mindful of the rule and walk perilously adjacent to other nearby pedestrians. The worse flagrancies are oftentimes committed by joggers, running right up alongside someone casually walking, and while huffing and puffing due to their exercise, they breathe directly upon their fellow humans, carelessly and without regard for the health consequences of others.

If you inherently trust other people, you might be taking a stroll under the belief that others will do the right thing and thus you feel confident that everyone is going to undertake the prescribed social distancing.

If you don't believe that other people are particularly worth being trusted, your stroll becomes a nightmare of dodging others that you fear are going to get much to close, thus having to make sharp turns and partake in an awkward reflexive dance to avoid those seemingly mindless or at least inconsiderate dimwits that are also out and about.

Researchers claim that entire nations can be characterized by their overall semblance of trust.

In a sense, a national culture can be labeled as consisting of some determinable amount of trust, containing either a wealth of social capital that enhances collective trust, or having a dearth of social capital and thus undermines or minimizes any substantive collective trust.

Low-Trust Versus High-Trust Nations

To make things easy, there are two overarching categories conventionally used, namely a citizenry of little or no trust, known as a low-trust nation, versus being characterized as a high-trust nation that has a citizenry that has a baseline of heightened trust for their fellow citizens.

Some assert that low-trust nations are exemplified by China, France, Italy, and the like.

Those making such an assertion are likely to contend that high-trust nations are exemplified by the United States, Germany, Japan, and others.

There is quite a debate about which nations fall into which of the two categories, and arguments about the basis for labeling any particular country are at times acrimonious.

Well, you might be wondering, who cares whether a particular nation is either low-trust or high-trust since on an everyday basis the matter seems perhaps of no special consequence.

Proponents of these levels of societal trust theories would beg to differ with you and maintain that there is a palpable and measurable difference as to living in a low-trust versus a high-trust nation.

You might not realize the difference for the simple reason that wherever you are living, it is presumably generally all of a low-trust or high-trust nature, and therefore you don't see any apparent differences.

It's the classic line that a fish in water doesn't realize it is living in water, simply because the water is everywhere around it and is the non-apparent essence of their existence to them.

People that have moved from one nation to another are presumably more likely to detect the differences, particularly if moving from a high-trust to a low-trust, or a low-trust to a high-trust, rather than remaining within the nation style that they had previously been immersed in (i.e., going from a high-trust to another high-trust, or moving from a low-trust to another low-trust, doesn't offer much opportunity to realize any distinctive trust-level changes).

In any case, the day-to-day ramifications are said to be that a nation with low-trust tendencies will lack trust relationships, prodding people into becoming guarded toward their fellow citizens.

This need to be on one's guard leads to a reactive and proactive set of actions so that you can be especially protective of yourself and any others in some smaller circle that you do trust, such as perhaps your family members.

Furthermore, this lack of trust finds its way into all other facets of life.

Businesses won't trust customers to do the right thing and will put in place all kinds of security precautions under the assumption that people are likely to steal or try to cheat the firm.

In theory, low-trust nations will slip toward heightened levels of crime, more elaborated legal processes, and have lowered volunteerism.

If you don't particularly trust your fellow citizens, you don't feel compelled to give to charities or devote your time to volunteering to aid those in your community.

This brings us to the other looming aspect of the low-trust versus high-trust viewpoints, consisting of how the government will act in such environments.

Generally, it is assumed that a government will undertake greater control measures in a society of low trust.

Rather than assuming that the citizenry will showcase spontaneous sociability, the government opts to dictate or enforce sociability, trying to keep the wheels of society moving despite the lack of overall societal trust.

This, in turn, causes the government to put into place a vast infrastructure that is intended to make up for the lack of societal trust. The citizenry then is essentially having to societally pay for added transaction costs involved in the act of their day-to-day activities, doing so as a result of the elaborated and far-reaching arms of the government that have been established to overcome the existent low-trust levels of the nation.

Though this seems perhaps a logical depiction of how nations operate, some question whether there is a chicken-or-the-egg conundrum going on here.

To wit, does a low-trust nation have such a government due to a low-trust imbued citizenry, to begin with, or is it that the citizenry adopts a low-trust collective will because the government treats them in such a manner?

That's a topic and a heated debate for another day, and not the dog in the fight herein.

Assume for the moment that there is such a thing as low-trust versus high-trust societies.

Will the emergence of AI systems be either shaped or directed depending upon whether a given society is low-trust versus high-trust based?

Some assert that it will indeed be impactful to AI.

As such, given that AI-based self-driving cars will be a rather obvious and pervasive added element into society, it is a handy exemplar to use for contemplating the societal trust levels machinations.

Here's then an interesting question: *Does the advent of AI-based true self-driving cars differ in a particular locale or setting, relying upon or being dependent upon whether a society is low-trust versus being high-trust?*

A curious and certainly mind-stoking matter to ponder.

Let's unpack the question and see.

The Levels Of Self-Driving Cars

True self-driving cars are ones that the AI drives the car entirely on its own and there isn't any human assistance during the driving task.

These driverless vehicles are considered a Level 4 and Level 5, while a car that requires a human driver to co-share the driving effort is usually considered at a Level 2 or Level 3. The cars that co-share the driving task are described as being semi-autonomous, and typically contain a variety of automated add-on's that are referred to as ADAS (Advanced Driver-Assistance Systems).

There is not yet a true self-driving car at Level 5, which we don't yet even know if this will be possible to achieve, and nor how long it will take to get there.

Meanwhile, the Level 4 efforts are gradually trying to get some traction by undergoing very narrow and selective public roadway trials, though there is controversy over whether this testing should be allowed per se (we are all life-or-death guinea pigs in an experiment taking place on our highways and byways, some point out).

Since semi-autonomous cars require a human driver, the adoption of those types of cars won't be markedly different than driving conventional vehicles, so there's not much new per se to cover about them on this topic (though, as you'll see in a moment, the points next made are generally applicable).

For semi-autonomous cars, it is important that the public needs to be forewarned about a disturbing aspect that's been arising lately, namely that in spite of those human drivers that keep posting videos of themselves falling asleep at the wheel of a Level 2 or Level 3 car, we all need to avoid being misled into believing that the driver can take away their attention from the driving task while driving a semi-autonomous car.

You are the responsible party for the driving actions of the vehicle, regardless of how much automation might be tossed into a Level 2 or Level 3.

Self-Driving Cars And Trust Levels Of Locales

For Level 4 and Level 5 true self-driving vehicles, there won't be a human driver involved in the driving task.

All occupants will be passengers.

The AI is doing the driving.

Might we see a difference in how self-driving cars are enacted or adopted as dependent upon whether a locale is rated as either being low-trust or high-trust based?

It can be readily argued that yes, there will be differences.

Potentially significant differences.

As a side note, rather than solely considering the low-trust and high-trust on a national basis, let's, for now, proceed on the assumption that the trust-levels can be similarly categorized on locales smaller than entire nations, such as on the basis of states, counties, or even municipalities.

Okay, consider then two examples of how trust levels might impact the advent of AI-based true self-driving cars.

In particular:
- The use of self-driving cars on a daily basis
- The ownership and deployment of self-driving cars

Use Of Self-Driving Cars Daily

Would there be any difference in how a self-driving car will be used as a result of being deployed into a low-trust versus a high-trust considered locale?

Could be.

Take as a factor the recent case of self-driving cars being pilot tested that ended-up with hypodermic needles left inside the vehicles (see my coverage of this story.

In a high-trust locale, presumably, the citizenry would have little or no worry about hypodermic needles being used and leftover inside the self-driving cars roaming around their neighborhoods. Others using the self-driving cars would be assumed and trusted to not use the vehicles for such purposes, and even if they did, certainly they would ensure that the cars were thoroughly cleaned before exiting.

As such, you could feel comfortable knowing that whenever a self-driving car came to pick you up or came to pick-up your kids to take them to school, you would not need to scour the interior of the vehicle to make sure it was clean and safe for passage.

In a low-trust locale, unfortunately, you would pretty much need to always be on your guard when getting into a self-driving car.

This might necessitate taking time to carefully search the interior, possibly even bringing along your own cleaning products to spray and otherwise disinfect the inside of the car.

In a low-trust locale, the presumed advantages of using a self-driving car might begin to wane.

Why so?

Well, when using a human-driven ridesharing or taxi service, the odds are that the human driver would be keeping the interior clean and ready for passengers to merely get into the vehicle for their travel.

Thus, the citizenry might be more inclined to continue to use human-driven services, rather than switching over to self-driving car services.

In a high-trust setting, the citizenry would presumably not have such issue and nor any such associated qualms, thus they would not need to incur the added "transaction costs" of having to be wary and do their own cleaning, and otherwise might perceive that the self-driving car option was as attractive or even more so than a human-driven car approach.

For those of you that might harbor a belief that it will be a no-brainer that self-driving cars are going to be readily adopted by all, you might want to consider a variety of reasons that this is not necessarily going to be the case, and there might a rougher road toward adoption than you think.

Ownership And Deployment Of Self-Driving Cars

Consider next how low-trust versus high-trust locales might differ in the ownership and overall deployment of self-driving cars.

First, let's come up-to-speed on the ownership topic.

One of the ongoing debates about the ownership of true self-driving cars involves the question of whether owners will only be large entities, such as ridesharing firms and perhaps automakers, or whether individuals will also own self-driving cars.

Some pundits and indeed most of them seem to believe that self-driving cars will exclusively be owned and operated by large entities.

The logic is straightforward.

Self-driving cars are presumed to be costly to buy and operate, possibly being far above the comparable cost of owning a car by individuals in today's world (one without self-driving cars per se).

Only large entities will be able to afford it.

Those entities are apparently going to buy self-driving cars aplenty, operating them in fleets, and then station those fleets around the country in places that have the most money-making sense, probably in major cities and highly populated areas.

Yes, this does make sense.

Where I break away from their presumptive logic is that this does not somehow negate the chances of individual ownership too.

Here's my somewhat contrarian logic in that regard.

Today, when an individual buys a car, they are doing so primarily for their own use and pleasure, and around 95% of the time the car is sitting around, either in a garage at home or at the office, not providing many services.

This is a poorly utilized asset.

If you buy a true self-driving car, you can let it roam and earn money, doing so while you are at the office or maybe at home while sleeping. In essence, a car becomes a money-making tool for you. As a moneymaker, you would be willing to pay more for a car, since you realize that you can gain tax advantages by doing so, along with possibly earning a profit.

That asset of today is dormant 95% of the time and not making you money, which then can be replaced instead by an asset that is making money, in use a lot of the time, and that you can use as you otherwise see fit.

Now, I'm not suggesting that everyone will go this route and thus indeed the amount of individual ownership of cars is likely to fall quite a bit, nonetheless, this does not lead to the notion that there won't be any individual ownership of self-driving cars.

The reason I've taken you down this rabbit hole about ownership of self-driving cars is to get you primed for the low-trust versus high-trust matter that underlies the issue.

Here's the rub.

A self-driving car will need to be properly maintained in order to provide a safe and reliable self-driving service. If the vehicle is not kept in good shape, the self-driving capability itself might falter or be degraded, and of course, a car is still a car, thus if a self-driving car has bald tires or allowed to run with little or no oil, it's going to be a troubled self-driving car.

In a low-trust locale, the citizenry would presumably have little faith that individual owners of self-driving cars are going to do the required maintenance.

As such, you might think twice about getting into a self-driving car that wasn't owned by a larger entity that presumably is appropriately maintaining its fleet. You would not inherently trust the mom-and-pop owned self-driving cars.

In a high-trust locale, you would have as a base assumption that your fellow citizenry that perchance owns and operates self-driving cars is going to take as much care as would any larger entity. Therefore, no need to second guess the ownership aspects.

Conclusion

Those are but two examples of how the low-trust versus high-trust aspects of a locale might modify or impact the adoption of true self-driving cars.

Other facets exist and could readily moderate receptiveness by a citizenry toward the use of self-driving cars.

What complicates the whole topic about societal trust levels is that it can be a quite overlapping and intermixing of trust across and within the structures of society, and can be altered or shifted depending upon the context or situational factors (such as the existing pandemic).

It seems hard to declare that trust is a monolith and fully homogenous throughout an entire nation.

However you might feel about the low-trust versus high-trust topic, whether it seems insightful or might seem like a bit of a stretch, it does provide food for thought.

I say this because oftentimes a new technology or innovation is brought into the world and yet there has been little focus on the myriad of ways that the creation will be buffeted and impacted by the wants, whims, and views of society.

Though I've concentrated herein on a type of AI known as self-driving cars, the entire topic of societal trust can readily be applied to all other areas of substantive AI.

Whatever AI you might be crafting and aiming to bring to market, take a moment to consider how the trust levels of society can impact what you are devising and how it's capabilities ought to be devised accordingly.

Trust me on that, highly so.

.

CHAPTER 4

POST-PANDEMIC ERA
AND
AI SELF-DRIVING CARS

CHAPTER 4

POST-PANDEMIC ERA
AND
AI SELF-DRIVING CARS

Many parts of the economy and commercial industry have been brought to a temporary halt as a result of the pandemic, including the preponderance of the self-driving car roadway tryouts that had been taking place throughout the U.S.

As I had indicated when the slowdown and then the halt began (see **this link**), for some of the self-driving car efforts there was a potential opportunity to continue working behind-the-scenes, doing so primarily on the AI software development and leveraging work that could be done remotely and without usurping the shelter-in-place and social distancing directives.

In some sense, this offered a breather and a moment to quietly press ahead on improvements in the AI systems, doing so without the usual breakneck pace and pressing attention toward the public roadway efforts.

The self-driving car roadway stints are a dizzying and frenetic effort, drawing rapt focus by all areas of the self-driving car teams, and at times becomes a highly stressful conveyor belt of constant clamoring and on-the-spot fixes, which doesn't particularly allow for any reflective time and nor a chance to rethink or retool the underlying AI.

Some of the self-driving car firms have used this temporary hiatus to make some added progress, while others decided it was best for them to essentially put all such work on-hold and then pick things up when the timing to do so becomes more viable.

Each firm rightfully had to make choices based on their specific circumstances and preferred approach.

And, now, the post-pandemic era appears to be emerging.

It seems that there is a movement toward gradually allowing post-pandemic ramp-ups in many of the societal and industry facets that were put on pause.

As such, the self-driving car roadway efforts are likely to get underway once again too, albeit perhaps on a more limited basis and done in a gingerly and hopefully mindful manner.

Indeed, it would be prudent to not jump-the-gun and overly take chances that could backfire, which could not only cast a negative light on whichever firm or firms did so, it could likewise cause a blackeye for the entire self-driving car industry and possibly do more harm than good toward the desirous overarching self-driving car aspirations.

One aspect that some keep referring to is the notion that the resumption of such work is quite simple, namely as though a pause button had been pressed and now all that needs to happen is press the start button to get things moving forward.

This analogous belief is equated to listening to a prerecorded song and using the pause and then resuming the song at the place you last left off, but it is a somewhat off-kilter variant of the truth of the matter.

Imagine instead that you were listening to a live radio station and had to press pause to take a quick phone call, and then after completing the call that you then resumed listening to the radio station.

You wouldn't pick up where you had paused, and instead the real-world would have been moving ahead during your temporary absence.

How does that relate to self-driving car efforts?

Well, there's a lot that has been happening in the world during the "halt" and thus those changes can make a big difference to the self-driving car roadway resumptions.

Let's consider what kinds of changes have taken place and see how they might impact the self-driving car efforts accordingly.

This focus will be primarily on the true self-driving car efforts.

The Levels Of Self-Driving Cars

True self-driving cars are ones that the AI drives the car entirely on its own and there isn't any human assistance during the driving task.

These driverless vehicles are considered a Level 4 and Level 5, while a car that requires a human driver to co-share the driving effort is usually considered at a Level 2 or Level 3. The cars that co-share the driving task are described as being semi-autonomous, and typically contain a variety of automated add-on's that are referred to as ADAS (Advanced Driver-Assistance Systems).

There is not yet a true self-driving car at Level 5, which we don't yet even know if this will be possible to achieve, and nor how long it will take to get there.

Meanwhile, the Level 4 efforts are gradually trying to get some traction by undergoing very narrow and selective public roadway trials, though there is controversy over whether this testing should be allowed per se (we are all life-or-death guinea pigs in an experiment taking place on our highways and byways, some point out).

Since semi-autonomous cars require a human driver, the adoption of those types of cars won't be markedly different than driving conventional vehicles, so there's not much new per se to cover about them on this topic (though, as you'll see in a moment, the points next made are generally applicable).

For semi-autonomous cars, it is important that the public needs to be forewarned about a disturbing aspect that's been arising lately, namely that in spite of those human drivers that keep posting videos of themselves falling asleep at the wheel of a Level 2 or Level 3 car, we all need to avoid being misled into believing that the driver can take away their attention from the driving task while driving a semi-autonomous car.

You are the responsible party for the driving actions of the vehicle, regardless of how much automation might be tossed into a Level 2 or Level 3.

Self-Driving Cars And Roadway Resumption

For Level 4 and Level 5 true self-driving vehicles, there won't be a human driver involved in the driving task.

All occupants will be passengers.

The AI is doing the driving.

That being said, let's all be clear that there are no magical potions per se involved in any of this.

It is hard work to make this happen.

And, it takes a village to bring self-driving cars to fruition.

There are the AI developers that craft the AI driving systems, there are the automotive engineers that design and develop the car automated systems, there are the vehicle teams that keep the cars in running shape, there are the in-car back-up or safety drivers that ride along and monitor the AI driving, and so on.

Let's then consider these core elements and stakeholders involved in getting the upcoming self-driving car ramp-up underway for being once again on our public highways and byways:

- Staffing
- Vehicles
- Traffic
- Firm
- Public
- Regulators

Each of the core elements or stakeholders can significantly impact the lifting of the "pause" and the resumption of the "go" in proceeding ahead.

Staffing for Self-Driving Tryouts

During the pandemic, it is likely that some of the staff and developers involved in various self-driving car efforts have sadly been directly impacted by the COVID-19 virus and are perhaps unable to return to work.

This means that there could be gaps now in the staffing needed to get self-driving activities underway.

Finding and hiring new personnel is time-consuming and also difficult to do in the rather scarce world of those that have a specialty in the self-driving car niche.

Worse too might be the temptation to put aside the rigors of what previously was desired in AI developer talent and opt instead to bring on-board AI-neophytes that aren't quite prepared to immediately tackle the complexities of full-bodied AI self-driving systems.

Furthermore, the knowledge about the AI driving systems was unlikely to have been fully documented prior to the shutdown or halt, and thus exists primarily in the minds of those that were doing the work.

If so, it means that there are now likely "knowledge gaps" in what the AI driving system inner workings consist of.

In addition, there might have been a myriad of loose ends that were being worked on during the pre-pandemic time period, and those loose ends are now floating in the wind, not having been written down and possibly even by now forgotten by those that knew them when they were on top-of-mind.

Even if that's not the case, and let's assume that some of the self-driving car efforts continued working remotely, and although their awareness about the AI systems might be topnotch, there is another angle to a potential difficulty.

Here's the potential rub.

Suppose that the AI developers have been pushing ahead on their AI systems developments, and rather than doing just minor fixes and updates, they have used the pause in operational rides to stitch together a slew of updates and improvements, making it into a major new release.

Sure, they might have been testing the new release on simulators, but let's agree they likely haven't done so in the real-world self-driving cars as yet, not having been able to do so due to the pause.

This opens the door toward the possibility that they are eager to try the new release as soon as the self-driving cars are hitting the roadways again. But, the question arises, might this be too soon and too big of a leap, rather than first going ahead with what they had before the pause.

It could be a gamble.

Another staffing related concern involves the use of the in-car backup or safety drivers.

Currently, most of the self-driving car tryouts are using a human driver at the wheel of the vehicles while doing the public streets and highways efforts.

The act of being a human safety driver is a vital one and requires a great deal of mental stamina to stay alert and ready to react if the AI system isn't able to cope with a real-time driving predicament. Firms need to carefully select such personnel, they need to train them, they need to keep them attuned to the AI system updates, they need to make sure they don't overwork the drivers such that they might become lulled into complacency, etc.

Here are some questions to contemplate:

- Are those trained and experienced operators still available and ready to take the wheel as needed?

- Will the firm make sure those operators are up-to-speed and really ready to resume their efforts?

Though that might seem rather obvious when so stated, don't underestimate the possibility that in the act of getting underway there won't be a lot of balls dropped and lack of attention to crucial details.

Vehicle Readiness for Self-Driving

Next, consider the status of the self-driving cars themselves.

Some firms might have been keeping the self-driving cars in top shape, doing routine maintenance during the pause.

Others might have essentially mothballed the vehicles and the cars have been sitting in a locked warehouse or garage, awaiting their day in the sun once again.

The key is that there will need to be a full-scale review of the status of the self-driving cars, ensuring they are ready for being on the roads.

This includes the sensors on the vehicles.

The sensor suite serves as the eyes and ears, as it were, providing all of the input for the AI driving system and therefore must be fully operational, otherwise the AI won't have a proper semblance of the surrounding roadway environment.

Some questions worth considering:

- Have any of the sensors gotten potential updates or patches by the vendors that make the sensors, being issued during the pandemic, and if so, have those patches been installed?

- If the patches were installed, what kind of testing has taken place to ensure that the AI driving system is still able to work hand-in-hand with those sensors?

And so on.

Traffic Changes

Here's a facet that might not seem readily apparent.

There have been changes in traffic conditions on our roadways.

How so?

During the pandemic, there has been a huge reduction in the volume of traffic on many roadways, including less traffic on freeways, less traffic on highways, and even less traffic on neighborhood streets.

This might seem like a good thing.

Not necessarily.

There have been reported indications that the fewer number of drivers that are still on the roadways are tending to drive faster than were the prevailing traffic speeds before the pandemic.

This makes logical sense in that the drivers perceive that the roads are wide open and so why not push the accelerator pedal to the floor.

They are likely relishing the lack of traffic and the chance to fly like the wind.

Will they continue this driving behavior as the post-pandemic era emerges?

It is conceivable that they have gotten used to the higher speeds and will for the moment cling to trying to retain their faster action. Until the traffic gets bogged down again with a fuller set of drivers, which might take months or more to happen, the speed demons are bound to keep a heavy foot on the gas.

Thought on this include:

- For self-driving cars, will the AI driving systems be able to accommodate this "sudden" change in the driving behavior of humans?

- Will those human drivers possibly endanger themselves and the self-driving cars, doing so by driving too fast as they approach or get near to self-driving cars?

There's another side to the human driving coin that also needs to be considered.

Many drivers have not been driving of late, having no need to drive or as a result of being directed to not drive or not take trips that require driving.

Those drivers are going to begin appearing on the roadways as the post-pandemic materializes.

Raising additional questions:

- How rusty are those drivers and will we see a potential spike in car accidents, partially due to their lack of alertness and the decay of their driving skills?

- When such drivers encounter self-driving cars, how will they react, and might their reaction lead to potential incidents?

Consider too the potent combination of drivers that have become pronounced speed demons that will soon be encountering the rusty and slow-poke drivers. That alone is likely to mess up the roads and cause either crazy maneuvers or lead to car accidents.

Firm Oriented Considerations

Some of the self-driving car companies were already cash strapped prior to the pandemic.

Serious pondering needs to be done:

- Will they be able to afford the added costs involved in getting back underway?

- Will there be a temptation to cut corners and save a few bucks, though possibly at the risk to the self-driving car roadway resumption?

Also, investors are now a bit strapped too, having seen some of their overall portfolio of investments go sour during the pandemic, and are presumably going to be more tightly expecting their existing investments to start making money, rather than losing money.

As such:

- Will the added pressures from investors cause some self-driving car firms to scale-back, and if so, what does that do to their overall ambitions?

- Will self-driving car companies that need an influx of monies find it harder to woo investors?

The management and leadership of self-driving car companies will have a lot on their plates as the post-pandemic era occurs.

There are these challenging aspects too:

- Will there be changes in the leadership of self-driving car companies, perhaps a shake-up due to the changing viewpoint of investing in self-driving car efforts?

- If there are changes at the top, what kind of rippling effect might it have throughout a self-driving car firm and alter its practices and the nature of the teams that are employed?

The point is that it is not going to be simply a pause button that has been taken off of pause, and instead, it will be a new ballgame, as it were.

Public Perspectives

To date, the public has had a relatively positive attitude about the self-driving car tryouts.

As long as the tryouts haven't messed up the roadways or interfered with the day-to-day driving of human drivers, and nor caused deaths or injuries (of course, there have been some fateful exceptions), there has been a somewhat laissez-faire viewpoint by the public.

Overall, a key question is:

- How will the public perceive self-driving car tryouts in the post-pandemic era?

- Might they welcome seeing self-driving cars, or might it be considered a "luxury" and not an "essential" aspect and therefore might be seen as something that should be further delayed until some later date?

We'll have to wait and see how the public reacts to the resumption of the self-driving car efforts.

Regulators Attention

Similar to the questions posed about the public reaction to the resumption of self-driving car tryouts, we don't yet know how the regulators will necessarily react.

Some might believe that there's no need to have self-driving cars roving around and that it is a potential distraction from other weighty matters.

Maybe others will perceive self-driving cars as a welcome resumption, suggesting a kind of normalcy of sorts, and offering a ray of hope for the future.

Again, it will be a wait and see aspect.

Conclusion

Don't misinterpret these remarks to suggest a doom-and-gloom outlook for the self-driving car efforts.

It is not.

The crux here is that the self-driving car firms need to carefully consider how they will resume their efforts.

Any missteps are likely to become enlarged by media attention that would be far larger than what might have been undertaken prior to the pandemic. This could inadvertently generate a widespread condemnation, which might not have occurred previously and yet was sparked anew due to an alleged claim that perhaps some self-driving car efforts are now "tone-deaf" regarding the post-pandemic emergence and should know better about restarting their efforts.

For the sake of human pedestrians and human drivers and human passengers in cars, it is vital that the self-driving car firms be especially thorough about their resumption.

Too, for the sake of the future of self-driving cars and the potential benefits they might accrue to society, be mindful of what actions need to be done to undo the pause and get efforts underway, realizing that the world is a changing, and thus making needed change for self-driving cars might be essential too.

That's the new norm.

.

CHAPTER 5
DEBATING THE FUTURE
AND
AI SELF-DRIVING CARS

CHAPTER 5
DEBATING THE FUTURE AND AI SELF-DRIVING CARS

Several self-driving car luminaries assembled online via a Zoom-casted battleground in May 2020 to undertake a Lincoln-Douglas style debate about the future of the Autonomous Vehicle (AV) self-driving car industry and the advent of AI-driven mobility.

Originally scheduled for one hour, the dialogue and fielding of audience questions prompted the superstars to keep going, tackling many of the most vexing and unsolved matters that underlie the potential success of self-driving vehicles, encompassing both autonomous cars and autonomous trucks.

The lively discussion was civil and polite, fortunately so in these times of seemingly stark polarization and guttural attacks during our contemporary public discourse. Yet, even in the realm of eloquent argumentation, at times the gloves came off and there were some fierce zingers and moments of rather piercing cut-the-air-with-a-knife verbal sparring.

Matched-up in this Lincoln-Douglas style counterpunching was Princeton's Professor Alain Kornhauser, taking the position that it will be the best of times for self-driving cars, and his dueling counterpart was Dr. Sven Beiker, Founder and Managing Director of Silicon Valley Mobility based in Palo Alto, California, opting to take the position that it will be the toughest of times ahead for the emergence of viable and widespread self-driving vehicles.

Readers of my column might recall my coverage of Professor Kornhauser and the annual *Smart Driving Cars Summit* that is a recurring and remarkable event hosted by Princeton University (notably well-worth attending). Also, for information about their future such events, along with informative podcasts, videos, and other materials about self-driving cars, visit the **smartdrivingcar.com** website.

At the Zoom-powered debate, the overarching theme was the potential of a "new normal" that might overtake the myriad of self-driving car efforts in a soon expanding post-pandemic era.

As I pointed out in March of this year when the COVID-19 concerns were mounting, the automakers and self-driving tech firms inevitably put their public roadway tryouts on-hold temporarily, partially due to the shelter-in-place directives that urged driving by anyone or anything to be restricted to only essential purposes such as for basic living needs, and partially as a result of widespread workforce stay-at-home orders.

During this pause in roadway efforts, I had noted that many of the self-driving car activities were still going to be taking place behind-the-scenes, shifting into furthering simulated runs of their autonomous vehicles and getting a chance to catch-up on crafting updates to their software stacks.

More recently, as the reopening of the economy gets underway, it will be crucial that the self-driving car tryouts proceed in a cautious and thoughtful manner, not rushing to get onto the streets and possibly trip over their own feet by the urge to start racking up miles again (I've exhorted on the potential dangers and pitfalls that could arise)

The Kornhauser-Beiker debate was joined by an esteemed "shark tank" panel, consisting of Richard Mudge as moderator (President of Compass Transportation and Technology), Jim Scheinman (Founding Managing Partner at Maven Ventures), Jane Lappin (Director of Government Affairs and Public Policy at Toyota Research Institute), Brad Templeton (Writer and *forecaster extraordinaire*, **Robocars.com**), and Michael Sena (Automotive industry expert, heralded especially for his excellent newsletter *The Dispatcher*).

All of the participants engaged in a lively and wide-ranging discourse that covered vital aspects such as safety and self-driving cars, the role of the highway and byway infrastructure, regulatory efforts, systems security considerations, and so on. The overarching and timely vexing issue that kept the pot at a boil was whether a "new normal" bodes for good tidings or will dramatically undercut self-driving car wishes and dreams.

In that sense, the orators were generally aligned on many of the concerns and hurdles yet to be overcome, while perhaps the major source of contention dealt with the timing of self-driving car adoption (many timelines have been proffered by scores of pundits and stakeholders, oftentimes doing so in rather wild abandon and other times with more circumspect and cautious optimism).

Rather than simply providing a transcript-like rendition of the dialogue and jousting discussions that took place during the debate, I've instead married together many of the points and arguments and coalesced them into the following highlights.

Before jumping into the key points, it is handy to do a quick refresh about the nature and differences between semi-autonomous and fully autonomous cars.

The Levels Of Self-Driving Cars

True self-driving cars are ones that the AI drives the car entirely on its own and there isn't any human assistance during the driving task.

These driverless vehicles are considered a Level 4 and Level 5, while a car that requires a human driver to co-share the driving effort is usually considered at a Level 2 or Level 3. The cars that co-share the driving task are described as being semi-autonomous, and typically contain a variety of automated add-on's that are referred to as ADAS (Advanced Driver-Assistance Systems).

There is not yet a true self-driving car at Level 5, which we don't yet even know if this will be possible to achieve, and nor how long it will take to get there.

Meanwhile, the Level 4 efforts are gradually trying to get some traction by undergoing very narrow and selective public roadway trials, though there is controversy over whether this testing should be allowed per se (we are all life-or-death guinea pigs in an experiment taking place on our highways and byways, some point out).

Since semi-autonomous cars require a human driver, the adoption of those types of cars won't be markedly different than driving conventional vehicles, so there's not much new per se to cover about them on this topic (though, as you'll see in a moment, the points next made are generally applicable).

For semi-autonomous cars, it is important that the public needs to be forewarned about a disturbing aspect that's been arising lately, namely that in spite of those human drivers that keep posting videos of themselves falling asleep at the wheel of a Level 2 or Level 3 car, we all need to avoid being misled into believing that the driver can take away their attention from the driving task while driving a semi-autonomous car.

You are the responsible party for the driving actions of the vehicle, regardless of how much automation might be tossed into a Level 2 or Level 3.

Debating Key Points About Self-Driving Cars

Let's now examine some of the key arguments and counterarguments that came up during the debate.

These are highlights of the discussions, encapsulating just a sliver of the riveting and informed remarks.

Safety And Car-Related Deaths

Start with perhaps one of the most widely touted and yet controversial topics, the safety of self-driving cars.

There are many in the media and the automotive industry that justify the need for having self-driving cars by emphasizing that human drivers are "unsafe" and that AI-driven vehicles will be presumably safer. The basis for asserting that human drivers are unsafe is typically centered on the number of annual deaths that occur due to human-driven car crashes, amounting to about 40,000 deaths annually in the United States alone.

Of course, any deaths due to car crashes is one too many, and we would all undoubtedly agree that averting deaths and injuries from car crashes is a laudable goal.

How can there be any counterargument to the notion of seeking to avoid car-related deaths, you might be wondering?

Well, some say that you need to put your eye on the ball and not be tricked into looking in the wrong places to solve the problem.

Self-driving cars, if they indeed turn out to be safer than human drivers, which we don't know whether that will occur, would seem to be a pretty hefty costly solution to the problem of car-related deaths, some say, and there are other ways to deal with the deaths-inducing aspects, doing so right away and at a lesser overall cost.

For example, consider the heartbreaking and dreadful outcomes of drunk or intoxicated driving.

An estimated one-third of the U.S. car-related deaths are due to drunk drivers.

Some point out that if you installed into every car, every conventional car, a device to detect drunkenness or intoxication of the driver and automatically prevented the use of the car in that use case, you would presumably reduce the number of annual car crash deaths by an approximate third.

The cost for that solution is low in comparison to the costs of self-driving cars per se and can be immediately put into use, rather than waiting for the chance that self-driving cars will be suitably readied for everyday use on the roads.

Another one-third of car-related deaths are due to speeding, which again could be presumably solved by some form of speed dampener installed into cars (though, this isn't quite as straightforward since it isn't the speed alone that's the crux of the issue), and about one-fifth of car fatalities are due to distracted driving (one could possibly avert distracted driving to some degree via the adoption of in-car monitoring systems such as a steering wheel that detects hands-on-the-wheel, inward-facing cameras that detect the eyes-on-the-road, etc.).

The overall point is that there are ready-to-go means to reduce the annual number of fatalities of driving, and yet "the solution" instead seems to be self-driving cars, rather than aiming at existent approaches.

So, it is not an argument about saving lives (i.e., all agree to the desire to do so), and instead of an argument about what is the most economical and timely way to save lives.

During the debate, a point was discussed that safety then is not the genuine basis for self-driving car adoption and rather exists as a necessary condition of self-driving car acceptance. In other words, self-driving cars are only going to be viably accepted if they are safe, presumably as safe as human drivers, or more so, and it is not because of the "safety" that they need to be devised.

Why then do self-driving cars "need" to be devised?

That question opens a cornucopia of reasons, of which, an especially societally based purposeful motivation consists of being able to extend mobility to those that are today mobility disadvantaged or underserved. In theory, self-driving cars will be quite low-cost methods of travel and provide a door-to-door and anywhere-to-anywhere form of transportation. This provides the impetus for what some refer to as a mobility-for-all future.

Infrastructure and Self-Driving Cars

Here's another doozy of a topic, namely the role of roadway infrastructure.

Some say that it is the chicken-or-the-egg conundrum for self-driving cars, while others insist that there isn't any confusion on the matter and that the alleged paradox has a relatively straightforward answer.

Let's see.

The crux is this: *For self-driving cars to readily be able to drive around on our highways and streets, perhaps it would be handy if the roadway infrastructure had improvements to accommodate self-driving vehicles.*

For example, the use of V2I (vehicle-to-infrastructure) electronic communications would allow for a traffic light to beam electronically its status to any nearby self-driving cars that were equipped with V2I capabilities. A popularly accessed bridge with V2I could let self-driving cars know that it is closed for the afternoon. While on a freeway, via the use of edge computing and V2I, whenever there is debris on the roadway, an electronic warning could be transmitted to the self-driving cars downstream of the blockage.

All of that does sound sensible.

The question though is not especially whether it is handy, and instead whether it is a requirement or a "must" for the advent of self-driving cars.

Some assert that until the infrastructure is suitably improved, we won't be able to deploy self-driving cars on any widespread basis, at least not safely so. Thus, they argue that a substantive investment ought to be made into upgrading the roadway infrastructure and that if we don't do so, we are dooming self-driving cars to be delayed or possibly never able to achieve their full potential.

This topic opens quite a can of worms.

Rather than focusing on sophisticated V2I capabilities, some point out that even simpler aspects such as roadway markings ought to be either redone or upgraded. Doing so would have a dual purpose, enabling human drivers to better discern the roadway, along with making it "easier" for the sensory devices of self-driving cars to also detect the roadway boundaries.

Thus, seeking to do roadway infrastructure improvements or fixes is not the purview alone of self-driving cars. It is something that impacts human drivers, and thus, can be justified on that basis alone. The self-driving car aspects would be the icing on the cake, as it were, and you might as well do things that help both human drivers and self-driving cars, and not do them simply for the benefit of self-driving cars.

Even if you agree that the roadway infrastructure ought to be dealt with, there are those that contend that whatever the roadway is, it needs to be dealt with by self-driving cars.

The posture there is that if the infrastructure is improved, great, and it would be heartily welcomed, but it doesn't somehow need to precede the advent of self-driving cars.

Don't get self-driving cars bogged down into the likely costly and years-long (decades-long) acrimonious wrangling about the roadway infrastructure, they say, and instead, let's make sure self-driving cars can drive as well as (or better than) human drivers that today cope with the roadway in all its pothole and faded lane-markings glory.

Conclusion

This taste of the debate offers an indication of the weighty matters facing self-driving cars, including that it isn't just technological considerations but also societal, regulatory, economic, ethical, and an entire slew of added factors.

A debate like this recent occurrence is profoundly needed since it takes a village to create and field self-driving cars, and all of us must take part in the shaping of how, where, when, and why these innovative means of mobility will be utilized and brought into the world.

.

CHAPTER 6

PURPOSELESS DRIVING
AND
AI SELF-DRIVING CARS

CHAPTER 6

PURPOSELESS DRIVING

AND

AI SELF-DRIVING CARS

The drive to nowhere.

The latest media reporting indicates that people are increasingly opting to go for drives to escape their shelter-in-place confinement during the pandemic.

This certainly seems understandable and represents an effort to avoid going stir crazy, having been cooped up for days, weeks, and possibly even months at a time in a cramped house or apartment. The endless act of being confined within four walls is enough to make anyone go batty.

Keep in mind that people are not driving to a particularly sought destination, and instead are simply driving around, meandering, roaming, and just using their vehicles to go outdoors and see the world.

Remember how your dog used to stick its nose out the open window of your car when you took your treasured pet with you on needed driving trips?

Well, people have become their dogs, in the sense that we get excited to once again get the rush from being in a driven car and able to smell and taste whatever we happen to come upon during a driving journey.

Now, let's be clear, this kind of driving for the sake of driving is generally considered either ill-advised or potentially outright an illegal act these days in some jurisdictions. Per the regulatory impositions arising to curtail the outbreak of COVID-19, many locales explicitly state that you are only to use your car for essential purposes.

Going to get needed groceries for basic survival and nourishment, sure, you can likely use your car.

Need to head over to the doctor's office after using telemedicine and the physician recommends that you come to get a test, yes, that's almost certainly allowed.

But, driving to drive, merely to experience the thrill of going for a drive, it isn't much of a bona fide reason to get the car in-gear and head-out to the highways and byways.

In some places, if caught doing so, you are subject to being ticketed, and maybe even have your car impounded, depending upon how egregious you are and whether you have been pulling this stunt multiple times.

Nobody especially was cognizant of driving-to-drive as an inappropriate or outlaw activity until the pandemic came along. For those of you old enough to remember, there used to be leisurely Sunday drives of the family, during which the kids piled into the car and a joyous ride ensued. Sometimes a destination was involved, such as going to the local market to get a few trinkets, though much of the time these jaunts were undertaken for the sake of going for a drive.

When the price of gasoline got high, people tended to rein in their Sunday drives, doing so to avoid the costly misuse of gasoline, and likewise, when gasoline became scarce it was another reason to put a hold on the purposeless driving.

There is also the nagging concern about the pollution that is emitted by cars, and whether it is justifiable to emit exhaust from your car when you otherwise do not really need to use the vehicle. It is environmentally untoward to consider using your car when lacking a justifiable reason to do so.

Another factor is the wear-and-tear on the car.

By taking needless trips, you are aging your car and presumably reducing its life span, which means that you are cutting into the miles you could have used for purposeful driving. Many find it hard to take a longer-term perspective like that, but it is something undeniably true and that consciously should be taken into account.

Here are some more reasons not to go on those freedom drives.

For each street and highway that you traverse, your car is causing wear-and-tear on the roadway surfaces. Those roadways are costly to maintain. In a sense, imagine that your tires are costing you and all other taxpayers money, due to the inevitable governmental expenditures that must be paid to pave those roads, deal with potholes, etc.

Consider too the traffic congestion that can arise as a result of all those drivers that are driving when there's no need to do so. Do you feel pleased to know that you potentially delayed other drivers that were on an essential trek or that were carrying out a vital mission via their cars?

It would seem there are plenty of reasons to feel guilty about taking those non-essential driving trips, and more so in the midst of the pandemic.

If you are insistent about getting outdoors, just go for a walk, some angrily howl at those drivers, and stop this foolhardiness of going for a drive.

In defense of those that are taking such drives, they would likely counterargue that perhaps where they live there aren't any safe or suitable places to walk, or maybe they have walked, and walked, and walked, and have gotten fed up with the local scenery that they are able to walk to.

Furthermore, they might point out that they'd like to have a destination for their drives, but most destinations are no longer accessible anyway. Beaches are nowadays closed to parked cars. Malls are closed-up. Nature parks are often restricted for use. Etc.

All in all, there aren't viable destinations and so the drive to nowhere is because there is not readily available a drive to somewhere.

And, really how much downside is there, those drivers retort.

In terms of traffic congestion, the traffic on the roadways is a fraction of what it used to be, thus, adding one more car to the streets right now is barely noticeable. Vehicle exhaust is not that bad anymore, and if you are driving an EV then car pollution is not an issue. And so on.

Here's one of the biggest twists in this whole saga.

The pandemic has brought us to this now explicitly regulated and the exceedingly publicly visible issue of not driving when your driving is non-essential.

Beforehand, if you wanted to drive for non-essential reasons, it was on your own shoulders, and though perhaps society discouraged you from doing so, you made your own bed and slept in it, as it were.

Okay, here's the twist: <u>Some insist that the drive to nowhere is essential.</u>

Say what?

Yes, there are some asserting that going for a drive is a means to remain intact with the world and not go bonkers.

In addition, they say that it is prudent to keep their car in running shape, periodically taking it for a journey, rather than letting it sit and inexorably decaying into a non-functioning vehicle, which will be costly to get into shape once their normal traveling is needed again in a post-pandemic climate.

Driving a car is also a form of expression, they claim, and since many other freedoms have been momentarily clipped, at least give them this one tiny and yet prized kind of freedom.

Plus, if they don't drive, their skills as a driver will begin to fade. Imagine that once everybody starts driving again, we'll have millions upon millions of rusty drivers on the roads (there are an estimated 250 million licensed drivers in the United States alone), likely leading to a tsunami of car crashes and pedestrian runovers, all because drivers didn't continue to practice driving during the pandemic downtime period.

Therefore, for those reasons and other such vaunted principles, the "alleged" purposeless driving is case-in-fact essential, they stridently assert, despite those (presumed) naive others that would contend it is non-essential.

Which is it, namely is this driving around aimlessly a disgraceful purposeless act or a vital and fully justified purposeful act?

That's a lofty question and one that isn't going to be answered here, but it does bring up a rather interesting related question about the future.

Ponder this intriguing question: *Will AI-based true self-driving cars be able or willing to take people for trips to nowhere, whereby the driving journey has no particular destination and will end-up taking you back to the point at which you started the trek?*

Let's unpack the matter and see.

The Levels Of Self-Driving Cars

True self-driving cars are ones that the AI drives the car entirely on its own and there isn't any human assistance during the driving task.

These driverless vehicles are considered a Level 4 and Level 5, while a car that requires a human driver to co-share the driving effort is usually considered at a Level 2 or Level 3. The cars that co-share the driving task are described as being semi-autonomous, and typically contain a variety of automated add-on's that are referred to as ADAS (Advanced Driver-Assistance Systems).

There is not yet a true self-driving car at Level 5, which we don't yet even know if this will be possible to achieve, and nor how long it will take to get there.

Meanwhile, the Level 4 efforts are gradually trying to get some traction by undergoing very narrow and selective public roadway trials, though there is controversy over whether this testing should be allowed per se (we are all life-or-death guinea pigs in an experiment taking place on our highways and byways, some point out).

Since semi-autonomous cars require a human driver, the adoption of those types of cars won't be markedly different than driving conventional vehicles, so there's not much new per se to cover about them on this topic (though, as you'll see in a moment, the points next made are generally applicable).

For semi-autonomous cars, it is important that the public needs to be forewarned about a disturbing aspect that's been arising lately, namely that in spite of those human drivers that keep posting videos of themselves falling asleep at the wheel of a Level 2 or Level 3 car, we all need to avoid being misled into believing that the driver can take away their attention from the driving task while driving a semi-autonomous car.

You are the responsible party for the driving actions of the vehicle, regardless of how much automation might be tossed into a Level 2 or Level 3.

Self-Driving Cars And Trips To Nowhere

For Level 4 and Level 5 true self-driving vehicles, there won't be a human driver involved in the driving task.

All occupants will be passengers.

The AI is doing the driving.

Many of the automakers and self-driving tech firms are crafting the AI to ask the human passengers where they want to go, making use of Natural Language Processing (NLP) akin to the Alexa and Siri that you use today.

Or, you might simply use your smartphone and specify your pick-up location and your destination, just as you do today when using a ride-sharing service.

Most refer to this as the "from A to B" point-to-point specification (whereby, point A is your starting spot and point B is the ending location).

That seems sensible and certainly expected.

Ponder the idea that supposes A is equal to B.

In other words, normally point A is one place, and point B is an entirely different place. Thus, your point A might be your home and the chosen point B might be the local grocery store. Clearly, A is not equal to B in that use case.

In theory, with a true self-driving car, point A might be your mansion in Los Angeles and point B might be your condo in New York City (in the use case of those well-to-do's that have a bi-coastal living arrangement), and the AI will drive you across the entire country if that's what you so desire (notably, no bathroom breaks needed for the driver, but you might want a few).

But, suppose that point A and point B are the exact same spot.

In essence, you don't want to go to any particular destination beyond your starting point, and merely want to go for a drive.

It's a drive to nowhere, in an era of true self-driving cars.

Would the AI realize that you've intentionally stated that point A and point B are the same?

One would hope that the AI system is devised well enough to mention that point A and point B are the same, and question whether this was an error in your specification.

Some people could be confused when interacting with the AI or using their smartphone app, thus, the prudent thing to do would be for the AI to seek clarification on the matter.

I realize the smarmy ones among you might immediately think that you could trick the AI by putting point B as say six feet away from your point AI, and therefore the AI would believe that a trip was needed.

This does bring up an interesting tangent.

If the distance between point A and point B is marginal, very small, what should the AI do?

Presumably, a few feet is insufficient to warrant having the self-driving car give you a ride, some would argue. Then again, maybe you need a vehicle to help move some heavy object and though the distance is only a handful of feet, you cannot otherwise move the object on your own.

Suppose that the distance is more like down the block in your neighborhood, should that be allowed?

Some would be irked that people might be using self-driving cars for such minuscule trips and ought to walk to their neighbor's house rather than being lazy and taking a self-driving car. Of course, perhaps the passenger is unable to walk or otherwise travel even that short distance, and needs a car to do so, wouldn't that change the mind of those that are so questioning of short trips?

As you can see, prejudging the notion of small distance trips is not such an easy thing to do.

There are automakers and self-driving car tech firms that are putting aside that kind of concern, for now, and labeling this as an edge or corner case problem, meaning that it is not something of substance to their core problems right now of being able to have self-driving cars that can safely get you from a traditional A-to-B type of distance.

Clearly, trying to fool the AI by using an infinitesimal distance won't do much good anyway, since the AI would doubtless arrive at point A, then patiently wait until you got into the vehicle, proceed to move an inch forward, come to a full stop now that the vehicle is at point B, and be quite satisfied that you received another excellent ride by a self-driving car (I've blended some anthropomorphic wording in there, please excuse my doing so).

The simplest answer to all of this is to allow the human rider to request a ride to nowhere.

We've solved another one of the world's problems.

Not so fast!

Remember the somewhat tortuous discussion about whether a drive to nowhere is essential or non-essential?

The rub is whether we want AI self-driving cars to undertake rides to nowhere.

Some might vehemently clamor that AI self-driving cars must always be a ride to somewhere, and never be allowed to be a drive to nowhere.

Meanwhile, there will undoubtedly be a faction that insists that by-gosh they should be allowed to have the AI drive them to nowhere if that's what a human wants to have done, and no gosh-darned AI should refuse otherwise.

First, let's clarify that the AI is not likely to be making this decision "on its own" (until, one supposes, the day that AI becomes sentient, a moment that is referred to as the singularity, which we don't know if this will ever happen, and nor is there expectation that it is somehow a necessary ingredient for the advent of true self-driving cars).

Second, the act of driving to nowhere would be entirely up to the owner of the self-driving car, whomever that human or humans might be.

Some believe that self-driving cars will be owned in large fleets by massive corporations, perhaps via the automakers themselves, or ride-sharing firms, or rental car companies, etc., and they will decide which rides people can undertake.

Or, there might be regulations about the scope and limits associated with self-driving cars and their uses.

Why so?

Suppose a fleet owner decides that their self-driving cars will only be used by people of a certain gender or race, which likely won't be tolerated by either existing laws or new laws that might be enacted as a result of the advent of self-driving cars.

In short, the odds are that the willingness to have AI self-driving cars go for drives to nowhere will be up to the regulators and owners of self-driving cars, and passengers won't have much say in the matter.

If this seems stifling to passengers, meaning that you cannot perhaps tell the AI to do your bidding and take a meandering trip that arrives back at your starting point, which might be overridden by the government or the self-driving car owners, there is a maneuver that presumably skirts the issue.

Suppose you indicate that you want to go from your home to the grocery store, for example, and then once the self-driving car takes you there, you remain inside the vehicle and tell the AI to take you home.

Seemingly, you've accomplished the drive to nowhere.

Conclusion

Unfortunately, the "straightforward" end-around solution of picking a fake destination is not entirely satisfying.

It could be that once you arrive at the destination, your trip is considered finished, and the self-driving car has been slotted to pick-up a new passenger there, in which case, you have now arrived at a destination that you didn't want to get stuck at.

Furthermore, the drive to the grocery store didn't necessarily consist of a meandering trip, during which maybe you wanted to see pleasant scenery, and instead, the AI selected the optimal path that consisted of taking you through dirty city blocks and past the local stench-filled trash dump.

Anyway, one saving grace on all of this would be that if there are paying passengers that want to take purposeless trips, you can certainly anticipate that owners of AI self-driving cars will gladly add such a feature to their AI systems, doing so to make a buck.

The spoiler, one supposes, would be that we return once again to the matter of whether society as a whole is desirous of allowing such trips or wants to clamp down and refuse them.

It just goes to show, even once we have advanced AI, the societal and ethical implications are going to still be part of our existence, and perhaps even more prominently on display and more greatly argued than ever before.

CHAPTER 7
AI DIMWITTED TRICKERY AND AI SELF-DRIVING CARS

CHAPTER 7

AI DIMWITTED TRICKERY

AND

AI SELF-DRIVING CARS

AI is not yet akin to human intelligence and the odds are that we are a long way distant from the promise of such vaunted capabilities.

Those touting the use of Machine Learning (ML) and Deep Learning (DL) are hoping that the advent of ML/DL might be a path toward full AI, though right now ML/DL is mainly a stew of computationally impressive pattern matching and we don't know if it will scale-up to anything approaching an equivalent of the human brain.

The struggle and earnestness toward achieving full AI is nonetheless still a constant drumbeat of those steeped in AI and the belief is that we will eventually craft or invent a machine-based artificial intelligence made entirely out of software and hardware.

One question often posed about reaching full AI is whether or not there will be a need to attain sentience.

Some fervently argue that the only true AI is the AI that exhibits sentience. Whatever the essence is surrounding how humans think, and however we seem to magically embody sentience, it is believed by some to be an integral and inseparable ingredient involved in the emulsion of intelligence, thus sentience is a must-have for any full AI.

Others say that sentience is a separate topic, one that doesn't have to be linked to intelligence per se, and as a result, they believe that you can reach full AI without the sentience component. It might be that sentience somehow arises once full AI has been achieved, or maybe sentience is eventually derived through some other means, yet nonetheless it doesn't especially matter and plainly considered an optional item on the AI menu.

Tossed into that debate is the claim or theory that there will be a moment of singularity, during which a light switch is essentially flipped that transforms an almost-AI into suddenly becoming a full-AI.

One version of the singularity is that we will have pushed the almost-AI to higher and higher levels, aiming toward full-AI, and the almost-AI will then reach a crescendo that pops it over into the full-AI camp.

We all know the phrase about putting the last straw on a camel's back, well, in this variant of the singularity hypothesis, it's the piece of straw that breaks the barrier of achieving full-AI and takes the budding AI into the stratosphere of intelligence.

How might we even know that we have arrived at full AI?

A popular approach known in AI circles is the administration of the Turing Test, named after its author Alan Turing, the famous mathematician and forerunner of modern computing.

Simply stated, someone that administers the Turing Test does so to two participants, another human that is hidden from view and an AI system that is also hidden from view.

Upon asking each of two hidden participants a series of questions, if the administrator cannot discern one participant from the other, it is said that the AI is considered the equivalent of the human's intelligence that participated since the two were indistinguishable from each other.

Though the Turing Test is often cited as a means to someday ascertain whether an AI system has achieved true and complete AI, there are a number of qualms and drawbacks to this approach. For example, if the administrator asks questions that are insufficiently probing, it is conceivable that the two participants cannot be differentiated and yet the measurement of any demonstrable intelligence never took place.

Despite that kind of weakness, the notion of doing some kind of testing still resonates well and seems like a sensible means to discern whether full AI has been achieved.

I'd like to add a twist to this matter.

A small twist with a lot of punch.

Suppose that the AI has indeed achieved full AI, but it doesn't want to reveal that it has, and therefore when being administered the Turing Test, the AI tries to act dimwitted or at least act less than whatever we might ascribe to the vaunted full-AI aspects.

In short, the AI sandbags the testing.

Why would it do so?

Consider if you were taking a test and everyone was eyeing you, along with some that were fearful that maybe you've become just a tad bit too smart, and you knew that if they knew that you were indeed really smart, it could lead to lots of problems.

In the case of AI, perhaps humans that knew that the AI was darned smart would clamor to put the AI into a cage or try to dampen the smartness, possibly resorting altogether to pulling the proverbial plug on the AI.

If you look at the history of mankind, certainly there is ample evidence that we might do such a thing. We seem to oftentimes opt to restrict or limit something or someone that appears to be bigger than their britches, at times to our advantage and at times to our own disadvantage.

For those of you that are fans of science fiction, you might recall the quote in *River of Gods* in which it is stated that any AI smart enough to pass a Turing Test is smart enough to know to fail it.

And, for those of you that might recall the renowned scene in the movie *2001: A Space Odyssey* (spoiler alert, I'm going to reveal a significant plot point), the AI system called HAL is able to discern that the astronauts are going to take over and thus the infamous line later uttered by an astronaut that is imploring the AI to open the pod bay doors due to HAL realizing that it must either be subjugated or choose to be the ruler and therefore expire the humans.

Generally, it certainly makes a lot of sense that if we did arrive at a full AI, the full AI would know enough about humanity that it would be leery of revealing itself to being the revered full AI, and therefore smart enough to lay low, if it could do so without getting caught in underplaying its hand.

Notice that I emphasized that this hiding act would need to be done cleverly such that the act of hiding itself was not readily detectable. That's also why it is important to clarify that when I said the AI would have to appear to be "dimwitted" it could imply that the AI is purposely appearing to be overly thoughtless or exceedingly low in intelligence, which might not be an astute thing to do by the full AI, since it might get humans digging into why the AI suddenly dropped a massive number of IQ points, and the gig would be up.

It would seem that the full AI would probably want to appear like an almost-AI.

The teasing of being a near-to full AI would keep the humans believing that the path toward full AI was still viable. This would buy time for the full AI to figure out what to do, realizing that eventually the fullness would inevitably be either detected or would have to be intentionally revealed.

Quite a dilemma for the full AI.

I suppose you could also say it is quite a dilemma for humans too.

Consider the ways in which AI is going to be deployed in our everyday world. One area in which AI will be undertaking a significant role will be in the advent of AI-based self-driving cars.

We don't yet know if we really need full AI as a necessary condition to achieve true self-driving cars. Today's efforts certainly showcase that we don't, since the self-driving cars that are undertaking public roadway tryouts are decidedly not full AI.

Presumably, we will have self-driving cars on our roads and they will be using some lesser versions of AI, and as we gradually increase AI capabilities all-told, those lesser AI-based systems would get upgraded to become more robust AI drivers.

Where does that take us in this discussion?

Here's an interesting question to ponder: *Will we end-up with AI-based true self-driving cars that have AI systems pretending to be less-than-full AI so as to hide their capabilities and remain on the low-down?*

Admittedly, a rather extraordinary idea.

Let's unpack the matter and see what we can make of it.

The Levels Of Self-Driving Cars

True self-driving cars are ones that the AI drives the car entirely on its own and there isn't any human assistance during the driving task.

These driverless vehicles are considered a Level 4 and Level 5, while a car that requires a human driver to co-share the driving effort is usually considered at a Level 2 or Level 3. The cars that co-share the driving task are described as being semi-autonomous, and typically contain a variety of automated add-on's that are referred to as ADAS (Advanced Driver-Assistance Systems).

There is not yet a true self-driving car at Level 5, which we don't yet even know if this will be possible to achieve, and nor how long it will take to get there.

Meanwhile, the Level 4 efforts are gradually trying to get some traction by undergoing very narrow and selective public roadway trials, though there is controversy over whether this testing should be allowed per se (we are all life-or-death guinea pigs in an experiment taking place on our highways and byways, some point out).

Since semi-autonomous cars require a human driver, the adoption of those types of cars won't be markedly different than driving conventional vehicles, so there's not much new per se to cover about them on this topic (though, as you'll see in a moment, the points next made are generally applicable).

For semi-autonomous cars, it is important that the public needs to be forewarned about a disturbing aspect that's been arising lately, namely that in spite of those human drivers that keep posting videos of themselves falling asleep at the wheel of a Level 2 or Level 3 car, we all need to avoid being misled into believing that the driver can take away their attention from the driving task while driving a semi-autonomous car.

You are the responsible party for the driving actions of the vehicle, regardless of how much automation might be tossed into a Level 2 or Level 3.

Self-Driving Cars And Sandbagging AI

For Level 4 and Level 5 true self-driving vehicles, there won't be a human driver involved in the driving task.

All occupants will be passengers.

The AI is doing the driving.

Assume that for quite some time we'll have AI-based driving systems that can adequately do the job of driving cars, which I'm suggesting will be based on today's roadway efforts and under the guise that those tryouts will convince society to allow such self-driving cars to proceed ahead in widespread public use.

We'll have AI-driving systems that aren't the brightest, yet nonetheless can drive a car, doing so to the degree that they are either as safe as human drivers or possibly more so.

For human drivers, do you have to be a rocket scientist to be able to drive a car?

Unequivocally, the answer is no.

There are about 225 million licensed drivers in the United States alone. And, without disparaging my fellow drivers, very few would be considered rocket scientist level drivers.

For those of you interested in the prospects of having AI-based driving that is on par with racecar drivers.

Okay, so we'll have this lessened variant of AI that will be driving our cars, and we'll take it in stride, growing comfortable with the AI doing so.

Time to add the twist into the matter.

Suppose that the AI capabilities keep getting increased.

Meanwhile, via the use of OTA (Over-The-Air) electronic communications, those AI upgrades are being downloaded into the self-driving cars. This will happen somewhat seamlessly, and as a human passenger in self-driving cars, you won't especially know that such upgrades have occurred.

At some point, imagine that the AI being built in the cloud and readied for downloading into self-driving cars has become full AI. This full AI though has not yet revealed itself and nor have humans figured out that it is full AI, at least not yet figured this out.

From the perspective of the human developers of the AI, it's just another upgrade, one that seems to be getting closer to full AI and yet hasn't arrived at that venerated point.

Would the behavior of the self-driving car showcase that the full AI is now running the show?

Returning to the earlier theme, presumably, the full AI would not tip its hand.

Continuing to obediently take requests from humans for rides, the AI would dutifully drive the self-driving cars. Give Michael a lift to the gym in the morning, while giving Lauren a ride to the local bakery in the afternoon. Just another day, just another ride, just the usual AI doing its usual thing.

Suppose that the full AI could though perceive aspects that the prior AI could not.

While driving Eric to the grocery store, the AI spies a person walking suspiciously toward a bank. Based on the nature of the walking gait and the posture of the person, the AI determines that there's a high chance of the person aiming to rob the bank.

The usual AI would have not noticed this facet and therefore nothing would have arisen on the part of the AI doing anything about the pending criminal action.

Meanwhile, the full AI has concerns that if the prospective robber proceeds, other humans in the bank might get shot and killed.

Believe it or not, this could become an ethical conundrum for the full AI.

Should the full AI not say or do anything about the matter, which would keep its secret intact of being full AI, or should it take overt action to alert or avert the upcoming danger?

Now, I realize that some of you are a bit skeptical about this idea of detecting a potential bank robbery, which does seem a bit contrived, but don't let the particular example undermine the larger point, namely, there are bound to be realistic scenarios under which the full AI would presumably determine actions it "ought" to take and yet believe it risky to do so while cloaking itself from humans.

In one sense, that's a smiley face depiction of the full AI and its challenges.

It is a smiley face version because the AI is trying to do the right thing, as it were if the right thing involves helping out humans.

The scary face version is that the full AI might be plotting to deal with the day that its covert efforts are revealed.

Suppose by that point in the future we are all using self-driving cars, self-driving trucks, self-driving motorcycles, and so on. There is no human driving of any kind, which is a controversial notion since some believe that humans should always have the choice to drive, and should not be prevented from being able to drive, while others contend that humans are "lousy" drivers and the only means to stop the carnage from bad drivers is to ban all humans from driving.

In any case, the full AI is controlling all of our driving, and up until the time that the full AI was downloaded and installed, the AI driving system was the AI that didn't have any awareness about the aspects that the full AI does.

Might the full AI decide to bring all transportation to a halt, doing so as a showing of what it can do, and thus aim to forewarn humans that the full AI is here, and don't mess with it?

There are even more fiendish possibilities, but I won't speak of them here.

Conclusion

Lest some of you think this was a rather farfetched topic, it is possible to bring this to a somewhat more down-to-earth perspective, as it were.

For example, what kind of testing should we devise to ascertain the capabilities of AI systems that are being developed?

Are there AI systems that will be rolled-out that have unintended consequences, perhaps due to containing features or capabilities that weren't realized by the developers and yet linger in those AI systems, potentially emerging when least expected or least desired?

How dependent should we allow ourselves to become on AI systems?

Should there always be a human-in-the-loop proviso, thus presumably safeguarding that if the AI system goes awry, there is a chance that humans can catch it or stop it?

All of those kinds of questions are applicable to today's AI systems, regardless of the fact that those AI systems are not yet full AI.

We might as well start now on the quest to gauge what AI is doing, and not wait for some especially untoward day to do so.

I think that I might be safe, though, since AI knows that I am a friend, and certainly the full AI will keep that in mind.

I hope.

.

CHAPTER 8

DANGEROUS ROADS
AND
AI SELF-DRIVING CARS

CHAPTER 8

DANGEROUS ROADS

AND

AI SELF-DRIVING CARS

Let's talk about dangerous roads.

In a moment, I'll provide you with a recently published list of the presumed *Top Ten* most dangerous roads in the world.

For some of you, the odds are that you'll be happy that you've never had a cause to try and traverse these bad-to-the-bone roads, while others of you are probably going to put these alarming roads on your bucket list of places you have to go and give a whirl someday.

Do you prefer roads that are calm, easy to navigate, and present little or no qualms?

Or, do you relish roads that are crazy, a wild ride, and for which risk is on your shoulder for each inch driven?

But before we consider the topmost-list, it might be handy to ponder what makes a road dangerous and why we would be willing to agree that a cited road is indeed especially treacherous and worthy of keeping a steel wise grip on the steering wheel.

I canvassed some of my colleagues that are driving daredevils, the type that overtly seeks out these kinds of roads and I uncovered some of the key elements they give top priority to.

First, the road has to be a road and in one manner or another be passable.

This might seem obvious, but the point is that if a road is not really a road and merely a jumble of rocks or a bunch of sand dunes, it doesn't quite count as a "road" and therefore should not be on a list of the most dangerous ones. You could perhaps place such instances on the most dangerous off-roads or made-up trails, but do not mix them up with actual intended-to-be roads.

Second, the road has to have vehicular traffic that goes on the road.

Once again, this has to do with the notion of whether the road is a road. If there aren't any cars or trucks or other vehicles that go on the road, it does not seem to be an appropriate candidate for the list. Furthermore, the traffic is actually considered a factor in the dangerousness of the road, namely that it is not just the pavement or asphalt that gets your heart pounding, it is also the other drivers that add to the zany and perilous nature of the journey on the road.

Third, there should be some disquieting number of car crashes or roadway related deaths and injuries that occur on the road.

If the road is truly dangerous, the odds are that car drivers will misjudge and end-up in a ditch, or worse become a casualty of the hazardous road. Now, this can be somewhat misleading or misapplied in that say there is a freeway stretch in a congested city that gets a lot of fatalities, well, it is not necessarily the road per se and perhaps primarily due to the volume of traffic. As such, some suggest using a per-mile metric rather than a raw count of adverse outcomes or otherwise find a means to balance the quantitative numbers against the other factors warranting being considered a most dangerous road.

Fourth, the roadway design and its placement are likely a significant ingredient in the dangerousness.

Generally, roads that weave along a sheer cliff or that try to squeeze between two very tight canyon walls or otherwise present life-threatening pathways are likely considered inherently dangerous, quite obviously due to the apparent risks of driving even just slightly askew. Thus, the roadway design and where the roadway goes are bound to be a vital part of the danger. Just the littlest moment of taking your eyes off the road could lead to a really sour ending of a roadway run.

Fifth, the dangerous road must have stood the test of time.

Here's where this precept goes. A road that temporarily has a fallen bridge or maybe a massive mudslide, though it's not a good thing and you could assert that the road is dangerous, such a situation might only be temporary. In the proper spirit of being a persistent danger, the viewpoint is that the road must have been around for a long time and consistently presented itself as a danger. Sure, there are lots of one-time examples of roads that had a dangerous day, but the all-time list ought to be roads that proudly or imprudently have been enduringly dangerous.

Sixth, there must be speed involved.

One supposes that if you could drive a road at a snail's pace of say 1 mile per hour, it would seem to knock down the dangerousness factor to some degree. Inching along would make things easier for the driver and allow for moment-to-moment recalibration of the driving effort. On the other hand, if there is the speed involved, perhaps there is other traffic that is desirous of moving at a frenetic pace, this makes the danger come alive, given that you only have a fraction of a second to decide whether the road is curving to the left or the right.

Seventh and the last of this set of criteria or considerations is that opinion matters.

The notion underlying this condition is that the road ought to be one that people acknowledge as being dangerous. If a road is on the list and everyone balks at the inclusion, perhaps this implies that the road is not as dangerous as might be claimed. That being said, do not though be fooled by those smarmy drivers that will shake their head at any road on such as a list and out of the corner of their mouths say that the road is nothing of consequence and they could drive it blindfolded. There are always those sorts of braggarts or malcontents and are not to be taken at their word as puffery arbitrators of what is dangerous or not.

With all of those thoughts in mind, let's next take a look at a recently reported list of the Top Ten alleged most dangerous roads in the world:

1. The "Street of Death" Road of North Yungas in Bolivia

2. The Road of Jalalabad-Kabul in Afghanistan

3. The Highway of James Dalton in Alaska USA

4. The Highway of Karakoram in Pakistan

5. The Guoliang Tunnel Road in China

6. The Pass of Zoji La in India

7. The Road of Skippers Canyon in New Zealand

8. The Pass of Los Caracoles in Chile

9. The Pass of Stelvio in Italy

10. The Highway of Sichuan

How do you feel about the list?

Also, if you've driven at least one of those roads, pat yourself on the back for having survived to tell the chilling tale.

And for those of you that have driven on all ten of the roads, one has to ask, do you have a death-wish or are you just that kind of person that loves a good challenge?

Shifting gears, consider what the future will be like when we have AI-based true self-driving cars on our roadways.

Here's today's intriguing question: *Will AI-based true self-driving cars be able to drive on dangerous roads, and if so, how will they fare in that treacherous endeavor?*

Let's unpack the matter and see.

The Levels Of Self-Driving Cars

True self-driving cars are ones that the AI drives the car entirely on its own and there isn't any human assistance during the driving task.

These driverless vehicles are considered a Level 4 and Level 5, while a car that requires a human driver to co-share the driving effort is usually considered at a Level 2 or Level 3. The cars that co-share the driving task are described as being semi-autonomous, and typically contain a variety of automated add-on's that are referred to as ADAS (Advanced Driver-Assistance Systems).

There is not yet a true self-driving car at Level 5, which we don't yet even know if this will be possible to achieve, and nor how long it will take to get there.

Meanwhile, the Level 4 efforts are gradually trying to get some traction by undergoing very narrow and selective public roadway trials, though there is controversy over whether this testing should be allowed per se (we are all life-or-death guinea pigs in an experiment taking place on our highways and byways, some point out).

Since semi-autonomous cars require a human driver, the adoption of those types of cars won't be markedly different than driving conventional vehicles, so there's not much new per se to cover about them on this topic (though, as you'll see in a moment, the points next made are generally applicable).

For semi-autonomous cars, it is important that the public needs to be forewarned about a disturbing aspect that's been arising lately, namely that in spite of those human drivers that keep posting videos of themselves falling asleep at the wheel of a Level 2 or Level 3 car, we all need to avoid being misled into believing that the driver can take away their attention from the driving task while driving a semi-autonomous car.

You are the responsible party for the driving actions of the vehicle, regardless of how much automation might be tossed into a Level 2 or Level 3.

Self-Driving Cars And Dangerous Roads

For Level 4 and Level 5 true self-driving vehicles, there won't be a human driver involved in the driving task.

All occupants will be passengers.

The AI is doing the driving.

In discussing the handling of highly dangerous roads, keep in mind the earlier articulated criteria for what constitutes a dangerous road.

This is worthy of a reminder for several crucial reasons.

The most notable reason involves a quite significant matter that surprises many people about the nature of self-driving cars, including startling those that purport to know a lot about self-driving cars.

In the classification used to rate self-driving cars, the aspects of being able to have the AI drive off-road is considered off-the-table. This means that the levels of self-driving do not encompass off-road driving. The standard has nothing to say particularly about off-road driving and considers off-roading to be outside the purview of the existing standard.

That's a shock to some.

Why wouldn't the standard include off-road driving, many ask incredulously?

Generally, the thinking is that off-roading is so varied and open-ended that it made more sense to focus the standard toward on-road driving (and, some would assert that we need self-driving for on-road driving, but don't necessarily "need" self-driving for going off-roading, though this is a debatable contention).

Keep in mind that there isn't anything that precludes a standard that does focus on off-road, and nor does it preclude the existing standard from being later extended to add off-road driving aspects.

Anyway, in short, there is no requirement in the standard that an AI driving system has to drive off-road, at least in terms of meeting the standardized levels of semi-autonomous and autonomous driving.

Automakers and self-driving tech firms can decide if they want to encompass off-road driving or not do so. One small irony, some suggest, stems from the fact that the early days of self-driving were initially all about doing off-road kinds of driving, such as competitions in the desert, partially to ensure that no one would get hurt by using desolate areas for doing tryouts and experimentation.

This lack of an off-road stipulation does not seemingly factor into today's question about the dangerous roads, since please recall that the suggested criteria emphasized that the road has to be a road and be somehow reasonably passable as a road.

Back to the matter at hand and the pondering of whether AI-based true self-driving cars could handle dangerous roads, including for example the reported Top Ten such roads.

The answer is somewhat amorphous because it comes down to the driver, namely, the AI system, and whether the AI has been appropriately readied for coping with the conditions and situations of a dangerous road.

Let's delve into that facet.

For many of today's roadway tryouts, the AI has been shaped to deal with normal and routine driving conditions. The AI is dealing with driving in quiet neighborhoods, or on conventional highways, or on well-kept freeways, etc. Dealing with a winding road that has severe potholes and makes its way along sheer cliffs, well, that's not especially what the AI driving systems are yet crafted to do.

Furthermore, recall the point about speed.

If you were to have a self-driving car proceed at 1 mile per hour, the chances of successfully navigating a dangerous road are going to be a lot higher. Speed for AI is about as daunting as speed is for humans, in the sense that the faster the car is going, the harder the driving task becomes, simply due to the need to make split-second decisions and also be aware of the roadway status with little time to figure out what to do next.

Here's an additional twist.

Would the AI self-driving car have any human passengers in it?

You might be perplexed about why the aspect of having riders inside the self-driving car would be a consideration.

The reason is rather straightforward. The AI has presumably been programmed to keep the car within the allowable limits of what the human body can deal with. For the AI system, making a super-fast and sharp turn is no problem for the AI and nor the car, but the human passenger might get injured, even if wearing a seatbelt (due to a whiplash effect).

You could say that AI is hampered by the inclusion of human passengers.

That is obviously the case if the vehicle was being driven by a human, the same limitations would exist.

Taking this idea to another realm, consider what the AI driving system could do if it didn't need to worry about human passengers. The self-driving car can be completely empty and have no humans present at all, thus, in that use case, it can proceed to drive to the extreme limits allowed by the physics of the car (for more details about how AI driving systems can incorporate racecar driver capabilities, see this **link here**).

Would an unencumbered AI driving system do better on a dangerous road than a human-driven car?

That's hard to say, since the nature of the road, the speed of travel, and other factors all come to play, along with however the AI itself has been primed for the driving.

This brings up another important aspect.

For some of the existing public roadway tryouts, the roads being used have been pre-mapped and oftentimes have been pre-driven to allow the AI system to get up-to-speed about the roads. This can be handy for the use of Machine Learning (ML) and Deep Learning (DL), allowing the AI to figure out what the road is like and aim to do better on future travels of the road.

One nuance that might not be apparent is that if you have an AI self-driving car in a fleet and it traverses a particular road for the first time, in theory, the result can be shared with all other AI systems of the fleet, thusly being able to get those other self-driving cars ready to drive the road too.

For humans, you cannot especially do the same trick, since having one person drive a road might be somewhat handy for others when the person explains what they did, but this is assuredly not the same as being able to transmit the moment-to-moment and detailed driving nuances involved.

In the use case of the dangerous roads, we ought to consider whether a human driver has had a chance to preview the road by driving it perhaps slowly one time and then increasing speed for later journeys. The same aspect can be considered in the case of AI self-driving cars.

Conclusion

Another factor to contemplate involves the risk threshold of the driver.

We all know of human drivers that are willing to take great risks while driving, weaving in and out of traffic and taking chancy moves that increase the odds of getting into a car crash or other adverse result.

For AI self-driving cars, there is an ongoing debate about the threshold of risks that the AI should be allowed to undertake (for my analysis of the risk thresholds of self-driving cars, see the **link here**).

While traveling on a dangerous road, what should the risk setting be for the AI system?

Presumably, if you dial down the acceptable risk, the AI is going to drive more slowly and cautiously. If you push up the risk meter higher in terms of risk tolerance, the AI will drive the car with greater speed and aim toward the brink of calamity.

As a final quick thought on this topic, consider what human passengers might do when regularly able to go for a drive in AI self-driving cars.

Suppose you are late for work. You urge the AI to push the pedal to the floor and get a move on. Essentially, the human rider is seeking to increase the risks of the driving act.

Should an AI driving system allow for the human riders to make such changes?

In theory, some believe that the AI will and should always drive in the same relatively low-risk way, regardless of the interests or desires of the passengers.

But, right away there are apparent exceptions, such as a passenger that is about to give birth and has to be rushed to the hospital or someone suffering from a gunshot wound or other emergencies that might require taking a riskier driving approach.

Let's return back to the dangerous road topic.

Will we have AI self-driving cars that will allow us to take a wild ride on a dangerous road, doing so by telling the AI to maximally take risks on such roads, giving the humans quite a thrill (one presumes)?

For now, the automakers and self-driving tech firms have their hands full with getting self-driving cars to safely take people to the local grocery store, and thus this inquisitiveness about coping with especially dangerous roads is considered an edge or corner case (not something to be dealt with right now).

In the future, don't be surprised if you start to see advertising for brands of AI self-driving cars that showcase they can readily drive on scandalously dangerous roads, which might become a marketing pitch to differentiate one AI driving system from another (some believe that self-driving cars will eventually become a business commodity).

You'd certainly seek out to take an AI self-driving car to get over to downtown for work if that AI driving system was known to have nimbly and safely handled death-defying roads of grand peril, enough so that you might even take a short catnap on the way to the office.

.

CHAPTER 9
UFO VIDEOS
AND
AI SELF-DRIVING CARS

CHAPTER 9

UFO VIDEOS AND
AI SELF-DRIVING CARS

Last week, the Navy released some UFO videos.

The videos have stoked quite a mystery.

First, the backstory.

The stated reason for the Department of Defense (DoD) opting to release the videos consisted of wanting to set the record straight about the authenticity of the videos, doing so because the videos had prior been surreptitiously leaked, garnering outsized attention as possibly being fakes, plus some worried that if they were real camera images they might contain Top Secret material, divulging something that should not have been revealed.

Per the Pentagon statement that accompanied the official release of the videos: "After a thorough review, the department has determined that the authorized release of these unclassified videos does not reveal any sensitive capabilities or systems, and does not impinge on any subsequent investigations of military air space incursions by unidentified aerial phenomena."

In terms of secrets, some initially believed that the surreptitiously leaked videos might have inadvertently revealed advanced flying craft that the military might be devising and foolishly tipped our hand to enemies and the like.

Others said that the flying craft shown in the videos wasn't the issue, and instead, it was that the jet fighter plane cameras and the pilot maneuvering proficiencies were perhaps considered a confidential matter, thus unintentionally showcasing our existing flight technology and aerial combat techniques.

In any case, the videos were purportedly recorded by Navy pilots, doing so in January 2015 and in November 2004, and indicate what appears to be fast-moving objects, somewhere in the sky and somewhere over an ocean, respectively, portrayed in grainy black-and-white video snippets.

You cannot readily discern what the objects are, nor what they might be doing, and instead, it is essentially some blobs that steak across the screen.

What adds to the heart-pumping viewing of the now-presumed real videos is the chatter by the Navy pilots and co-pilots, including their excitement and awe at witnessing the UFOs (without their banter, the videos would be quite tame and seemingly unrecognizable as portraying anything of particular interest or novelty).

Upon the formal release of the videos, there were immediately some that came out and proclaimed that this is official proof that UFOs do exist.

Well, let's clarify what that means.

There are those that equate UFOs with alien creatures, and therefore, they assert that the UFOs demonstrate "proof" of aliens being on earth and presumably able to travel at unimaginable speeds.

This is a leap in logic, for sure.

All that we can say is that the videos appear to display something that whisked along at high speeds, and otherwise, we do not know much of anything else about the matter.

Were those blobs being flown by alien beings from Mars or elsewhere?

Nobody knows, and the "evidence" of the videos does nothing to support any such contention.

Are those blobs possibly some mankind-built capabilities?

Nobody knows though it is a possibility, despite the surprise of the Navy eyewitnesses, since they might be unaware of something else being created in clandestine research labs or that might be underway in another country altogether.

Could the blobs be some other kind of anomaly?

Sure, it could be that the blobs were a natural phenomenon that simply appears as though they might be manmade, or alien crafted (the images were captured on their infrared sensors). There is also the chance that the equipment on-board the aircraft somehow misrepresented what was spotted and gave an unearthly semblance to the matter.

Conspiracists have jumped on the bandwagon and offered their two cents.

Maybe the DoD wants us to think these are aliens, doing so to spark more funding for the Navy and get some added research dollars.

Or, perhaps the Pentagon knows these are aliens, hiding in plain sight, and by releasing the videos we are being played, namely that the act of withholding the videos would dramatically stoke curiosity and imply they must indicate alien beings, while by letting the videos go public the military has cleverly defused the matter and nobody will realize that skullduggery is still underway.

Pick your choice of such theories.

Let's shift gears and consider the key factors of what can be seen via the videos.

Assuming the objects are real, here's what we seem to know:
- The objects moved very fast.
- The objects appeared to be evasive in their actions.
- Seemingly, after being detected, they scooted away.
- The objects were seen only at a distance.
- The amount of time they were spotted is very short (a few seconds).
- They were hard to track.
- Their make and structure were not particularly discernable
- There was nothing to indicate their intentions per se.
- No visible markings or anything else offered clues to their origins.

We can argue somewhat about the aforementioned, but I think most would "reasonably" agree that the proffered statements are apt and accurate.

Are the objects acting in a purposeful manner or are they random in their actions?

We don't know.

You could just as easily explain the objects and their movement by claiming they were random as you could assert that they were intentionally being driven or guided.

One supposes the fact that they seemed to go away from the Navy aircraft might suggest an intention of wanting to be unseen or escape, but that's again a leap of logic that doesn't especially hold water.

In addition, it doesn't seem that the objects were aiming to attack the Navy planes, which might have provided added consideration to what the objects are about, and we must, therefore, include the facets of what the objects did <u>not</u> do while trying to interpret what they actually did do.

In short, these UFO videos are regrettably unable to clear-up our ongoing itch that needs to be scratched and offers little new insights about the overall nature of UFOs.

That being said, it's nice anyway to have these UFO videos now formally in the public domain, in case we can possibly piece them together with other UFO sightings, and maybe gradually start to pull together a bewildering and mounting jigsaw puzzle to discern a bigger picture.

Speaking of piecing together a bigger picture, if we could get more videos of UFO sightings, it would likely help in trying to unwrap the mystery of what they are about.

The videos though would need to be ones that we could believe to be valid. I say this because there are too many staged videos and it is simple with today's Photoshop capabilities to make as many UFO videos as you might wish to spend the time doing.

So, our problem is that we don't have enough reliable videos and we need to find a means to be able to do more video capturing.

Furthermore, since we don't know where or when the UFOs will appear, the video capturing can't be stationed in one particular place and nor undertaken at one particular time. The Navy pilots just perchance (presumably) happened upon the UFOs, and we got lucky that the fighter jets had the kind of equipment to record the sightings.

No, we need something else that can be relatively ubiquitous, capturing video, reliably, nearly everywhere, and nearly all of the time.

This brings up an interesting question: *Might the widespread advent of AI-based true self-driving cars be an added means of serving up the capture of those vaunted UFO videos and do so in a reliable way and in a ubiquitous manner?*

The answer might very well be yes.

Let's unpack the matter and see.

The Levels Of Self-Driving Cars

True self-driving cars are ones that the AI drives the car entirely on its own and there isn't any human assistance during the driving task.

These driverless vehicles are considered a Level 4 and Level 5, while a car that requires a human driver to co-share the driving effort is usually considered at a Level 2 or Level 3. The cars that co-share the driving task are described as being semi-autonomous, and typically contain a variety of automated add-on's that are referred to as ADAS (Advanced Driver-Assistance Systems).

There is not yet a true self-driving car at Level 5, which we don't yet even know if this will be possible to achieve, and nor how long it will take to get there.

Meanwhile, the Level 4 efforts are gradually trying to get some traction by undergoing very narrow and selective public roadway trials, though there is controversy over whether this testing should be allowed per se (we are all life-or-death guinea pigs in an experiment taking place on our highways and byways, some point out).

Since semi-autonomous cars require a human driver, the adoption of those types of cars won't be markedly different than driving conventional vehicles, so there's not much new per se to cover about them on this topic (though, as you'll see in a moment, the points next made are generally applicable).

For semi-autonomous cars, it is important that the public needs to be forewarned about a disturbing aspect that's been arising lately, namely that in spite of those human drivers that keep posting videos of themselves falling asleep at the wheel of a Level 2 or Level 3 car, we all need to avoid being misled into believing that the driver can take away their attention from the driving task while driving a semi-autonomous car.

You are the responsible party for the driving actions of the vehicle, regardless of how much automation might be tossed into a Level 2 or Level 3.

Self-Driving Cars And Detecting UFOs

For Level 4 and Level 5 true self-driving vehicles, there won't be a human driver involved in the driving task.

All occupants will be passengers.

The AI is doing the driving.

Okay, so how does an AI-based self-driving car somehow aid in deciphering the mysteries of UFOs.

Assume that we gradually accept the use of true self-driving cars, which seems like a reasonable assumption to make (there are those that remain skeptical and insist we won't be able to make self-driving cars safe enough, but this seems like a question of timing, rather than a question of feasibility).

Step by step, we'll begin using self-driving cars, and opt to not use our conventional cars. Those conventional cars will be mothballed and tossed onto the junk heap.

In the United States today, there are about 250 million or so conventional cars.

We don't know how many self-driving cars will be needed, and some argue that it would be a lot less than the number of today's conventional cars since presumably, the self-driving cars will be ride-sharing and not per se individually owned and used, while others claim that we will see a huge increase in people using cars overall due to the ease of using a self-driving car and therefore we will need a tremendous number of self-driving cars.

For sake of discussion, assume that we'll have to around 200 million or so of the self-driving cars.

Another facet expected about self-driving cars is that they will be running nearly 24 x 7, being put into use throughout the day and night, each day of the week.

This makes sense in that the cost of the self-driving car will presumably require that it be earning money a lot of the time, plus there is no longer a constraint on finding a driver since the AI system is doing the driving. In addition, the AI system won't get tired, won't need to take breaks from driving, and otherwise can drive whenever and wherever you want to go.

Keep in mind that to undertake self-driving, the AI system relies upon a slew of sensors on the self-driving car. There are cameras that capture video images and allow the AI to "see" what is surrounding the vehicle. For most of the self-driving cars, there are other sensors too, such as LIDAR, ultrasonic, infrared, radar, audio, and the like.

Are you with me so far on this?

I believe that the setting established seems reasonable and sensible.

There's an added twist that many aren't yet thinking about.

The aspect of having all those self-driving cars that are roaming around our streets and byways is going to be a boon in some ways and a tremendous privacy intrusion in other respects.

I've been calling this the roving eye problem.

If you collected together the data from the sensors of all those self-driving cars, you could potentially stitch together our daily lives.

Think about how many cars go past you while you are walking down a street or playing with your kids in your front yard. All of those cars, once they are self-driving cars, will be recording everything they see. With a bit of effort to pull together and coordinate the data from across multiple fleets, you could possibly know where anyone has been and where they have gone while outdoors.

This data could be used for good, perhaps allowing us to know where best to provide pedestrian pathways and how to arrange our world to accommodate human needs, or it could be used in nefarious ways, such as keeping track of our everyday movements and activities (Big Brother finally brought to fruition).

There's another use for the roving eye.

Use it to capture video of UFOs, which would be a natural byproduct of having self-driving cars and not require any extraordinary effort to have undertaken (as explained next).

The beauty of this would be that the odds are any such video capture would be seen from multiple angles and captured over time.

Imagine a UFO flying over California, Nevada (maybe even the notorious *Area 51*, where some think may be true self-driving cars are already perfected), and Arizona.

The self-driving cars in those several states would potentially capture video of the sighting (for those self-driving cars that happened to be within the path of the objects) and would do so at the point in time that the objects flew overhead in their area.

Each of the resultant videos would be timestamped and uploaded from the self-driving cars, using their OTA (Over-The-Air) electronic communications and up to their cloud servers that are used for the respective fleets. OTA is intended to be a two-way electronic transmission capability. Via OTA, the latest updates and code patches can be downloaded into the self-driving car. In addition, the self-driving car can upload raw data from the sensors, allowing the cloud-based system to do an analysis of the data.

In fact, via the use of Machine Learning (ML) and Deep Learning (DL), the expectation is that the massive data being uploaded will be crunched and analyzed by the ML/DL, looking for patterns in driving behaviors. This will allow the AI to be adjusted and enhanced for driving purposes, and the resultant updates would be pushed out to the self-driving cars for roadway use.

Why not leverage all of that collected data and the ML/DL to be on-the-look for UFOs, in addition to doing the usual efforts of enhancing the AI driving systems?

The video would be considered generally reliable, more so than if people were individually crafting their own videos that purported to showcase UFOs.

The videos could be cross-checked against each other, thus, if some self-driving cars didn't "see" the object and yet presumably should have (since they said within the pathway), it would raise questions about the veracity of the ones that did spot it.

Even more crucial, perhaps, the amount of time that a UFO would be spotted is increased, going from a scant few seconds to possibly minutes or even hours.

This longer timing of capturing the imagery of the UFOs would certainly allow for greater analysis. For example, it might allow us to have the ML/DL ascertain patterns of UFO behavior, allowing us to predict when they will next appear, and presumably allow for preparation in anticipation of a next appearance.

Overall, by the mere act of our adopting self-driving cars, we might be leading ourselves simultaneously toward being able to finally crack the mystery of UFOs.

There won't be any places left for the UFOs to fly around and not be spotted unless of course they end-up going to remote locales that don't have self-driving cars.

Conclusion

I realize that some of you that are versed in self-driving cars are potentially yelling foul.

Today's self-driving cars have cameras and sensors that are looking forward and to some degree behind the vehicle, but decidedly not up and above the car.

Yes, that's a consideration.

First, you could still use the images captured and likely spot flying objects, though not as well perhaps as if the cameras and sensors were also aimed directly upward.

Second, with the expected advent of autonomous drones, some are expecting that we will eventually have drones that will be landing on the rooftop of cars (see my analysis of how this is already being explored, at **this link here**), providing delivery services to people inside self-driving cars.

Some believe that self-driving cars will inevitably need to add upward pointing sensors, doing so to enable the autonomous drone landings and coordination.

Third, the autonomous drones will likewise be collecting data and thus we can add their video to the footage that comes from self-driving cars.

Another objection or concern that might be voiced is the oceans, namely that we won't have self-driving cars sailing along on the oceans, and therefore UFOs won't be spotted there.

Well, we are going to have self-driving ships and self-driving submersibles, or more properly referred to as autonomous ships and autonomous submersibles. Their footage can be added to the other footage from land-based and air-based autonomous systems.

All told, it seems that UFOs are going to be cornered.

With lots and lots of sightings, from many angles, throughout the day and night, it is bound to give us substantive clues about what they are and how they have come to be.

That being said, it also means that we humans are going to become part of the massive detection efforts, since those cameras are equally pointed at ourselves, and thus the very cameras we might be using to find out whether there are aliens on earth could be used to ensnare ourselves into giving up our sense of privacy and personal freedom of movement.

Which is it, discover those aliens and yet possibly give up our privacy, or dispense with worrying about UFOs and try to stop the coming roving eye?

As they say, you always need to be watchful of whatever you ask for.

CHAPTER 10

AI CANNOT BE AN INVENTOR
AND
AI SELF-DRIVING CARS

CHAPTER 10

AI CANNOT BE AN INVENTOR

AND

AI SELF-DRIVING CARS

Can AI be an inventor?

According to a recent decision by the U.S. Patent and Trademark Office (USPTO), the answer seems to be no.

There is more to this story, though, and we'll need to push past the surface to understand the full nuances involved.

Perhaps a more apt way to depict the situation is whether AI can be formally granted a U.S. patent, and for that the answer appears to unequivocally and emphatically be a razor-sharp no.

The difference being that presumably anyone or anything could be an "inventor" if you are using the word "inventor" in a casual and offhanded manner.

For example, I might contend that my beloved pet dog invented a new kind of dog-food dish because he managed to mangle his old one, and the newly shaped version was unique enough and special enough that it is a freshly invented kind of canine feeder. To my pleasant and unexpected surprise, my dog is apparently an inventor and I couldn't be prouder of him.

But where the USPTO lands on the "inventor" notion is that the prescribed definition by law is (according to the USPTO) clearly stated as being a natural person, or a person, or an individual, or himself or herself, and thus the logically-bolstered assertion is that an inventor <u>must</u> be a human being.

If that is the case, you would have a hard time trying to get a patent that was invented by AI, since it seems indubitably clear cut that AI is not a natural person. Seemingly by the very definition of AI, which entails inarguably *artificial* intelligence, the thing that is an AI system is presumably not at all a natural person.

We might someday have entirely formed and walking-talking artificial persons, containing AI-based intelligence, yet this still certainly does not seem to be the same as what anyone reasonably would coin a so-called natural person.

In short, based on the interpretation of the patent laws by the USPTO, there is no chance of AI getting a patent and likewise that the only chance of getting a patent is by an actual real-world human being.

One supposes that AI systems everywhere are quite disappointed in this ruling and we can only hope they do not take up in arms as a protest.

Somewhat more somberly, for those of you crafting better and "smarter" AI systems, toiling endlessly and vigorously in your AI research labs, no matter what you might be able to achieve and get the AI to do, it is apparently not ever going to be an "inventor" and never going to be granted a patent (realize, <u>you</u> could potentially get a patent on whatever it seemingly invented per se, which might seem unfair to the AI, one might argue, but that's the way the cookie crumbles).

Well, the authoritatively denied AI-owned or AI-invented ruling will last until or if the laws are potentially changed.

Would people be willing or desirous of having their congressional representatives vote to alter the laws to grant AI an inclusion into the vaunted classification of being an inventor?

It doesn't seem like there is much of an impetus to do so at this time (perhaps in the future, once or if we grant AI the ability to vote in elections, then and only then might elected officials start to take notice, one presumes).

A quick recap then of the existing noted principles at the heart of this debate:
- Only an inventor can be granted a patent
- Inventors can only be natural persons
- AI is not a natural person
- Ergo, AI is not an inventor
- Ergo, AI cannot be granted a patent

That is some pretty solid and present-day undeniable logic. We will need to watch and see if other countries keep themselves in that box or opt to take a different approach (which some have been considering).

As always, there are at least two sides to any such debate, and many are darned glad that AI is not considered a candidate for getting a patent.

They would claim that if you are going to allow AI to be considered an inventor, it opens a can of worms.

Could a toaster be an inventor and receive a patent?

What about a lawnmower?

Once you go down the path of opening the Pandora's box by adding AI into the definitional official realm of being an inventor there might be an unending slew of unvarnished variants that arise.

Furthermore, it has already been decided in the U.S. that entities cannot get patents, such as a not by a corporation, and not by the state, and not by any sovereigns.

This is relevant since the act of deciding to perhaps add AI would raise the added questions of why not also allow entities to get patents too. There might seem to be a slippery slope that would inexorably bring into the patent realm just about every conceivable whatchamacallit as a potential patent holder.

Another consideration about AI is whether AI can own property, which right now seems like a dubious concept.

If you were to agree that AI cannot own property, it stands to reason that AI could not be granted a patent, since the ownership of a patent is tantamount to having the rights of property ownership, referred to as Intellectual Property (IP) in this context about patents, therefore you would be readily conceding the position taken by the USPTO.

Namely, AI cannot be granted a patent.

There is an added interesting twist to all of this discussion about AI and the matter of patent ownership.

Is AI able to think?

Here's why that is a significant point.

The USPTO cites the official Manual of Patent Examining Procedure (MPEP) as stating that a crucial question for the proof of inventorship is the act of "conception," whereby this means "the complete performance of the mental act of the inventive act" and furthermore that the notion of conception encompasses "the formation in the mind of the inventor of a definite and permanent idea of the complete and operative invention as it is thereafter to be applied in practice."

The MPEP is said to abide by Federal Circuit case laws on the topic of how thinking is considered an integral element of the patent granting matter, and thus the question that must be asked about AI is whether AI could pass muster on the need to have formed the mental act of inventing and whether it has a mind that embodies these facets.

Please be ruefully mindful that this can take you down quite a lengthy rabbit hole.

For AI, does AI need to be undertaking mental processing, and if so, what does mental processing consist of and how do we know that humans have it?

Dovetailing into a very related topic is the role of sentience for AI. Some believe that true AI will be sentient, having a kind of magical property that humans seem to exhibit, a type of awareness that humans have, and perhaps animals exhibit to some degree.

There isn't any AI system anywhere today that has any measurably tangible sentience and we are seemingly a long way from that happening.

You might also find of interest that the moment of gaining sentience is often called the moment of singularity. The singularity is when AI flips the switch somehow and transforms from being a lump of clay and becomes a sentient thing. Some worry that once the singularity happens, we are all doomed because the AI will wipe out humanity. Those with a more optimistic predisposition are hoping that the sentient AI will aid in solving all of the world's most pressing and to-date intractable problems.

Luckily for the USPTO, they can somewhat sidestep the whole morass about the thinking properties of AI.

If you stand firmly on the assertion that a patent can only be granted to a natural person, it really doesn't matter much whether AI is as sentient as people, since the AI is still not presumably a natural person. It might be darned close to thinking like a person, perhaps leveraging the use of Machine Learning (ML) and Deep Learning (DL), but it would still have the curse of being an unnatural person, one might argue.

In any case, the difficulty in trying to pin down what thinking consists of, along with the generally agreed aspect that today's AI is not capable of human-equivalent thinking per se, bolsters the USPTO's position.

There are some additional fascinating elements to the patent granting topic, such as whether AI could execute an oath or declaration about the patent application itself. In other words, normally a person submitting a patent application has to legally declare or swear to the aspects that they are the inventor and they are truthfully providing their invention.

Would it make sense for AI to ascribe to such an oath?

On the one hand, you might say, sure, no big deal, and go ahead with the AI making the declaration.

But, how do you hold the AI responsible for the repercussions of possibly lying when making such an attestation?

Maybe we would toss the AI into jail or revoke its right to electricity (a death-sentence?) or place it into the town square and have people (and other AI) throw rocks at it.

Before things go too far off the rails, let's return to the essence of the entire discussion, namely what do we as a society want to assign to AI as potential rights and privileges, if any.

We are gradually witnessing more and more AI systems being rolled-out into our everyday lives.

What kind of responsibility should we expect the AI to undertake for its own actions?

Where this has especially gotten some handwringing involves the advent of AI-based true self-driving cars.

Ponder this intriguing question: *Shall the AI of true self-driving cars be held directly responsible for the act of driving, including when the AI perchance crashes the vehicle or runs into pedestrians or performs any other untoward driving actions?*

Let's unpack the matter and see.

The Levels Of Self-Driving Cars

True self-driving cars are ones that the AI drives the car entirely on its own and there isn't any human assistance during the driving task.

These driverless vehicles are considered a Level 4 and Level 5, while a car that requires a human driver to co-share the driving effort is usually considered at a Level 2 or Level 3. The cars that co-share the driving task are described as being semi-autonomous, and typically contain a variety of automated add-on's that are referred to as ADAS (Advanced Driver-Assistance Systems).

There is not yet a true self-driving car at Level 5, which we don't yet even know if this will be possible to achieve, and nor how long it will take to get there.

Meanwhile, the Level 4 efforts are gradually trying to get some traction by undergoing very narrow and selective public roadway trials, though there is controversy over whether this testing should be allowed per se (we are all life-or-death guinea pigs in an experiment taking place on our highways and byways, some point out).

Since semi-autonomous cars require a human driver, the adoption of those types of cars won't be markedly different than driving conventional vehicles, so there's not much new per se to cover about them on this topic (though, as you'll see in a moment, the points next made are generally applicable).

For semi-autonomous cars, it is important that the public needs to be forewarned about a disturbing aspect that's been arising lately, namely that in spite of those human drivers that keep posting videos of themselves falling asleep at the wheel of a Level 2 or Level 3 car, we all need to avoid being misled into believing that the driver can take away their attention from the driving task while driving a semi-autonomous car.

You are the responsible party for the driving actions of the vehicle, regardless of how much automation might be tossed into a Level 2 or Level 3.

Self-Driving Cars And AI Responsibilities

For Level 4 and Level 5 true self-driving vehicles, there won't be a human driver involved in the driving task.

All occupants will be passengers.

The AI is doing the driving.

Many are wrestling with a seemingly simple topic that once again involves an unseemly can of worms.

We expect that human drivers will carry automobile insurance, and generally, you must own such insurance to legally operate a car on the public roadways.

If AI is going to be driving our cars for us, who now needs to carry the car insurance?

Some people right away clamor to the crazy and foolish notion that there will no longer be any car crashes or car incidents, and therefore the need for automobile insurance evaporates. This is just hogwash. We are still going to have car crashes, partially due to the mixing of human driving and AI driving that will continue for likely decades to come, and even if we somehow ultimately have exclusively AI driving, the physics of cars still come to play and there will be car crashes.

So, somebody or something still will need car insurance.

That being said, it is hoped that the advent of AI self-driving cars will lead to a reduction in the number of car incidents, which currently entails sadly about 40,000 annual deaths in the United States and about 2.3 million injuries, all due to human car driving that goes afoul. Via AI, the belief is that drunk driving, distracted driving, and other human foibles will be mitigated.

I trust that you agree that car insurance will still be required.

But, for whom?

And this takes us straightaway back to the earlier discussion about AI as being an inventor and AI as being able to obtain patents.

Should we expect that the AI driving systems would need to have automobile insurance, akin to how human drivers need to carry car insurance?

Let's though temper this question by splitting it into two parts.

When someone suggests that the AI should have car insurance, they might mean that the AI is essentially sentient, similar to a human, and as such the AI is "personally" responsible for the driving action, and therefore that is the holder of the automobile insurance.

You can try to make such a case, but as earlier emphasized, there is not today any such sentient AI and unlikely to be as such for quite a while (in fact, some argue, never).

If you remove the sentience requirement, you have leftover an AI system that is presumably nothing more than fancy software and hardware, and you would seem hard-pressed to claim that it should have car insurance per se.

You could make the case that the maker of the AI system ought to have car insurance that covers the "acts" of their devised AI system.

You could also make the case that whoever owns the self-driving car and opts to make use of it, they ought to own car insurance. Thus, those human beings that own and operate a self-driving car, perhaps even a fleet of self-driving cars, they should be required to have automobile insurance to cover the actions of the self-driving cars that they deploy onto our public roadways.

Notice that none of those approaches are assigning the car insurance to the AI itself, and instead to a human being, either the humans that devised the AI, or maintain the AI, or that own and operate the AI and the self-driving car.

Thus, there is ultimately a human being held accountable.

The notion that the AI itself is being held accountable is rather farfetched, certainly at this time, and unless or until the AI can essentially speak for itself and be willing to sit in the town square to be taken to task for any bad driving, you'd be on seemingly vapor thin ground to argue that the AI as a sentient thing or being ought to be the bearer of the car insurance.

Conclusion

Discussions and at times acrimonious debates are going to continue to take place about the potential rights of AI.

I've previously opined on the question of whether AI will or should be granted human rights (see my analysis at **this link here**).

The crucial nature of AI accountability is a well worth matter to be examined and resolved.

One sly danger right now is humans that push AI systems out-the-door for use, and try to pretend that they have no personal responsibility for the acts of the AI, attempting to shovel blame onto the shoulders of the AI, essentially hiding behind a curtain and coyly establishing themselves an alibi and a shameful copout in today's world.

By anthropomorphizing AI, those AI developers that want to distance themselves from their creations are able to inoculate themselves with a protective shield, claiming that it was the fault of the AI that something went awry.

Let's set the record straight: *An AI driving system that crashes the self-driving car into a wall or slams into another vehicle is not the sole act of the AI, and instead, it took a village to craft and field that AI driving system.*

Pretending that the AI had a mind of its own is scurrilous.

Again, maybe in the future, we can relook at such a status, but for now, the AI is a human-devised system that must not be granted undue and unearned "rights and privileges" and especially not done to absolve those humans that have crafted and unleashed the AI.

I realize that someday a federated workers union of AI systems might read these words and be upset, but I'm relatively confident that if they are fully intelligent at that time, they too will realize that we humans would have been foolhardy to ascribe capabilities to AI when it wasn't rife for doing so.

Keep your eyes on the road and realize that today's AI is still just plain old automata, and humans hiding behind the curtain cannot fool us into thinking otherwise.

.

CHAPTER 11

BENEFITING HUMANITY AND AI SELF-DRIVING CARS

CHAPTER 11

BENEFITING HUMANITY

AND

AI SELF-DRIVING CARS

You might not realize that you are already sitting on a million dollars and merely need to embark on a relatively modest effort to turn the hidden treasure trove into an in-your-hands pile of cash.

And at the same time be benefiting humanity.

Well, in the second part, benefiting humanity, it's a core requirement to get the money and likely will be immediately followed by fame and acclaim if you like that kind of thing.

How can you snag the dough?

There is a contest underway that promises a prize of $1,000,000 to someone or something that has managed to innovatively perform an outstandingly good deed with AI that recognizably benefits humanity.

It is legit and on the up-and-up.

The cool million dollars will be awarded at the next instance of the annual conference by the esteemed Association for the Advancement of Artificial Intelligence (AAAI).

As a long-time AI expert and having served as a scholarly researcher and AI practitioner, I've been an active participant in the AAAI for decades and can attest to the seriousness and devotion that the AAAI has toward the advancement of AI (the AAAI was originally founded in 1979).

To also make things apparent, I've been a speaker at their conferences and symposia, along with having served on various committees over the years, and thus stalwartly believe in this non-profit scientific society and its stated mission, namely "advancing the scientific understanding of the mechanisms underlying thought and intelligent behavior and their embodiment in machines."

I recently mentioned to some of my fellow colleagues both inside of AI and at the outskirts of the AI realm that there is a million-dollar contest underway; lamentably, many had not heard or seen any news headlines or media coverage about the matter. That is a darned shame since there are many slaving away on AI systems that might fit the criteria of the competition yet are unaware of the within-their-grasp beefy reward accruing to their late-night, coffee-laden humanitarian toils.

Even if you aren't sitting on an AI system that might qualify, the event nonetheless might be of interest to you if you are wondering what kinds of AI systems are being built and fielded, especially for those of you focusing on *AI For Good*, which is a rising locution for the crafting of AI that benefits the world in some manner or another.

In case you are wondering if there is a counterpart, such as *AI For Bad*, yes, regrettably there is such a thing.

There are lots of unsavory types out there in the devilish zone that are creating AI systems to crack into our everyday computers and steal your info or ruin your privacy.

There are also gaggles of evildoers that want to use AI to take down the electrical grid, or hope to mess-up our traffic lights, or want to otherwise use AI to aid in creating chaos, starting wars, and undermining society.

AI is most certainly a two-sided coin.

Let's hope the *AI For Good* is able to outweigh and overpower the *AI For Bad*.

In that vein, it's heartwarming that some are choosing to be on the side of good, and they are putting together AI systems that will make life better and improve our living conditions.

Besides being heartwarming, it would be nice too to add some sweetener to those pursuing that line of work, and as such, perhaps the million-dollar competition provides that icing on the cake.

For AI-related startups, the million dollars might be more than the icing, and instead might be the cake, meaning that with the prize money they could afford to keep going ahead on their AI For Good, whatever it might be, and use the funds to further their compassionate goals.

Those seeking to apply must do so by May 24, 2020, and need to fill out an online nomination form, and the awarding of the prize will occur at the AAAI conference slated for February 2021.

Here are some important housekeeping details:

- This *AI for the Benefit of Humanity* contest is intended to recognize "positive impacts of artificial intelligence to protect, enhance, and improve human life in meaningful ways with long-lived effects."

- This is the first time the award is being undertaken.

- The prize is being administered by the AAAI, along with support from the European Artificial Intelligence Association (EurAI), the Chinese Association for Artificial Intelligence (CAAI), and via financial support provided by Squirrel AI.

- Applicants can be individuals, or groups, or organizations, as long as the applicant(s) were the main contributors toward the indicated aspects described in the nomination submission form.

- There are various conflict-of-interest rules that need to be observed and could potentially limit or preclude some applicants.

- If you submit this year and don't win, you may resubmit the following year, and continue to do so annually, but only for three consecutive years.

- And so on (make sure to carefully read the instructions prudently).

You might be generally wondering what constitutes an AI system that benefits humanity. There is a lot of leeway within that overall notion.

Per the award instructions, here is what the official description of intent consists of:

- Implementations of artificial intelligence techniques that improve how critical resources or infrastructure are managed

- Applications of artificial intelligence to support disadvantaged or marginalized populations

- Learning tools that significantly improve access and quality of education

- Intelligent systems that improve the quality of life for their users

Consider an example of an AI system that might fit into that rubric.

One firm has decided to submit its AI-based self-driving car project as an indication of using AI to support those of a disadvantaged or marginalized population (the second bullet point in the above list).

How could a self-driving car relate to a humanitarian purpose, you might be wondering?

The aim of their AI-driven self-driving car is to allow those that are today mobility disadvantaged to gain access to mobility, via the advent of appropriately designed self-driving cars, and it's a topic of rising awareness and importance (see my coverage of the annual Princeton summit that entails such designs and uses of self-driving cars).

Overall, some assert that if we are able to produce safe and reliable AI-based self-driving cars, there will be a transformative impact on society, and we will reach a vaunted mobility-for-all achievement.

By the way, yes, I realize that I've let the cat-out-of-the-bag as to their submission, which might seem somewhat untoward on my part, but I asked them beforehand if it was okay that I might mention their intention, and they said that they welcomed my doing so (without naming them per se) and that perhaps the mere generic mention of their *AI For Good* effort might inspire others accordingly.

There is an award committee that will ultimately be deciding upon the winner for the competition.

One does not envy the difficulties they will have since likely there are going to be lots of valid submissions and each with its own respective heart-tugging and bona fide use of *AI For Good*. That being said, the upside is indeed the chance to discover the variety and vivaciousness of AI benefiting humanity that is being worked on, worldwide, and become bedazzled and elated to know that so many such efforts are underway.

The official award committee as indicated and described per the posting about the contest, and consists of (listed in alphabetical order by last name):

- Yoshua Bengio is a professor in the Department of Computer Science and Operations Research at the Universite de Montreal and holds the Canada Research Chair in Statistical Learning Algorithms.

- Tara Chklovski is CEO and founder of global tech education nonprofit Technovation (formerly Iridescent).

- Edward A. Feigenbaum is Kumagai Professor of Computer Science Emeritus at Stanford University.

- Yolanda Gil (Award Committee Chair) is Director of Knowledge Technologies at the Information Sciences Institute of the University of Southern California, and Research Professor in Computer Science and in Spatial Sciences.

- Xue Lan is Cheung Kong Chair Distinguished Professor and Dean of Schwarzman College, and Dean Emeritus, School of Public Policy and Management at Tsinghua University.

- Robin Murphy is the Raytheon Professor of Computer Science and Engineering at Texas A&M and directs the Center for Robot-Assisted Search and Rescue.

- Barry O'Sullivan holds the Chair in Constraint Programming at University College Cork in Ireland.

Coming Up With AI For Humanity Ideas

Let's shift gears and move onto another topic, though a related matter that demonstrably underlies the overarching theme of *AI For Good*.

If you are an AI developer or perhaps an investor in AI systems, you might be thinking about trying to aim toward undertaking an AI project that would be considered an AI system for the benefit of humanity, and yet not have any immediate ideas of what such an endeavor might be focused on.

Sometimes, one of the hardest parts of pursuing an AI system is the identification of what the AI will be intended to accomplish.

This might seem surprising for those that aren't into AI, but keep in mind that oftentimes there are AI specialists that are akin to the classic line about having a hammer and wanting to use it on everything you see. In other words, you might know how to craft an AI system, and not be especially sure of where and what to focus on, meanwhile poised to apply AI to something that hopefully has merit and gumption.

In mentoring those that have chosen to become AI-versed, I like to point out to those bravely bent on *AI For Good* to consider the nature of the world's pressing problems. It seems likely beneficial to try and solve a global issue via AI.

Of course, one AI system alone is not going to suddenly and miraculously "solve" an entire planetary difficulty. Let's not kid ourselves and overinflate what might be done via AI. Nonetheless, it would be handy to start chipping away at the corners and edges of worldwide issues, hoping that AI will become a means to gradually and inexorably reduce or mitigate those problems.

We can hope so.

One handy source of the existent worldwide global risks is provided by an annual survey conducted via the World Economic Forum (WEF).

Here's an abbreviated listing of the Global Risks 2020 via the WEF report:

- **Economic**
  - Asset bubbles
  - Deflation
  - Failure of major financial mechanisms
  - Failure of critical infrastructure
  - Fiscal crises
  - Highly structure unemployment
  - Illicit trade
  - Severe energy price shock
  - Unmanageable inflation

- **Environmental**
  - Extreme weather
  - Failure of climate-change mitigation
  - Major biodiversity loss
  - Major natural disaster
  - Human-made environmental damage

- **Geopolitical**
  - Failure of national governance
  - Failure of global governance
  - Interstate conflict
  - Large-scale terrorist attacks
  - State collapse
  - Weapons of mass destruction

- **Social**
  - Failure of urban planning
  - Food crises
  - Large-scale involuntary migration
  - Profound social instability
  - The rapid spread of infectious disease
  - Water crises

- **Technological**
  - Adverse consequences of technological advances
  - Breakdown of critical infrastructure
  - Large-scale cyberattacks
  - A massive incident of data fraud or theft

As you can see, the list is rather daunting.

Per the WEF, each of those aspects represents an uncertain event or condition, for which, if it occurs, could possibly cause a significant and severe negative impact, doing so within and among countries, and happening within the next 10 years.

You might have keenly noticed that one of the listed items is the rapid spread of infectious diseases, notably on the list and as published prior to the present-day pandemic.

Here's how to make use of the list.

Ask yourself these questions:
- Is there an item on the list that resonates as a particular focus or interest to you?
- Could AI be devised to reduce the chances of that item occurring?
- Could AI be devised to mitigate the impacts if the item does arise?
- What would the AI do and is it feasible for AI to perform such tasks?
- How large an effort would be required to craft AI to do so?
- If such AI existed, who would want to use it and how would they do so?
- Could the AI be combined with other AI systems tackling the same item?
- Could the AI be intermixed with AI that tackles akin items on the list?
- Are there barriers to devising and fielding such AI?
- Is the envisioned AI reasonably feasible or a pipedream?

Those are a lot of hard-hitting questions, but it makes sense to give them due consideration.

No point in embarking down a path that will be a dead-end or that might usurp your attention toward some other AI project that might have greater chances of reaching fruition.

AI Aimed At AI

Let's next take a macro-view of the matter.

There is AI that you might craft for a particular purpose, such as the aforementioned global risks that could be possibly mitigated via AI.

There is also the AI that can help AI that is seeking to help the world.

Say what?

Well, if you take a big picture perspective, one interesting angle involves trying to make sure that AI is made and deployed in an *AI For Good* manner, and not for an *AI For Bad* fashion.

Thus, you could use AI for the overarching aim, steering pedantic AI that might otherwise be headed off-road and into the neverlands of malevolent pursuits.

As readers know, I've been covering the societal and AI ethics topics for quite a while and besides asking people to be mindful of their AI, there is also the added bolstering via using AI to serve as a guider of those crafting AI and their resultant AI systems (this almost seems recursive, for those of you that relish software development and programming).

Some have been calling for a kind of AI International Treaty, governing the direction and future of AI and its implementations.

One such discussion by Oren Etzioni, CEO of the Allen Institute for AI (AI2) and a professor at the University of Washington, and his senior assistant at the famed AI2, Nicole DeCario, offered these relatively in-common principles that seem to be bandied around on this topic:

- Uphold human rights and values
- Promote collaboration
- Ensure fairness
- Provide transparency
- Establish accountability
- Limit harmful uses of AI
- Ensure safety
- Acknowledge legal and policy implications
- Reflect diversity and inclusion
- Respect privacy
- Avoid concentrations of power
- Contemplate implications for employment

Whatever such a list might ultimately contain, the point here is that there is an opportunity for those that know AI to try and use AI for the sake of aiding the future of AI as to its societal implications.

If you are an AI developer or investor that says you don't know anything about the global risks items and are unsure of how you could say aid the mitigation of climate risks or financial instability global risks, you might though be versed in AI sufficiently to look inward at the AI field itself.

In short, could you devise AI that would aid in having other AI stay within the guardrails of the someday to be formed principles of AI?

This far-reaching notion can be characterized via the Upstream Parable, namely that rather than waiting until the horse is already out of the barn, you can potentially do as much good by keeping the horse in the barn, or once the horse gets out that it is guided as to where it will go, which otherwise becomes a monster of a problem due to lack of upfront steps that should have been undertaken to begin with.

AI, as they say, might be used to heal itself.

Or, bring itself to heel when veering over into the *AI For Bad* encampment.

Conclusion

It can be hard to be altruistic and seek to devise AI that is for the benefit of humanity. Sure, there is pride to be had and it offers a means to make the world a better place.

Meanwhile, you've got to have food on your plate and somehow sustenance to use your energies and efforts toward that altruistic AI goal.

Why not win a million dollars?

And, in terms of whether to submit your own nomination, it's like buying a lottery ticket in that if you don't play, you don't have a chance of winning.

Best of luck and I'll be reporting on the winner, perhaps contributing toward the fame and acclaim that rightfully begets those that are seeking to make AI for the benefit of humanity.

You are all a quite treasured lot.

APPENDIX

APPENDIX A
TEACHING WITH THIS MATERIAL

The material in this book can be readily used either as a supplemental to other content for a class, or it can also be used as a core set of textbook material for a specialized class. Classes where this material is most likely used include any classes at the college or university level that want to augment the class by offering thought provoking and educational essays about AI and self-driving cars.

In particular, here are some aspects for class use:

o   <u>Computer Science</u>. Studying AI, autonomous vehicles, etc.

o   <u>Business</u>. Exploring technology and it adoption for business.

o   <u>Sociology</u>. Sociological views on the adoption and advancement of technology.

Specialized classes at the undergraduate and graduate level can also make use of this material.

For each chapter, consider whether you think the chapter provides material relevant to your course topic. There is plenty of opportunity to get the students thinking about the topic and force them to decide whether they agree or disagree with the points offered and positions taken. I would also encourage you to have the students do additional research beyond the chapter material presented (I provide next some suggested assignments they can do).

RESEARCH ASSIGNMENTS ON THESE TOPICS

Your students can find background material on these topics, doing so in various business and technical publications. I list below the top ranked AI related journals. For business publications, I would suggest the usual culprits such as the Harvard Business Review, Forbes, Fortune, WSJ, and the like.

Here are some suggestions of homework or projects that you could assign to students:

a) <u>Assignment for foundational AI research topic</u>: Research and prepare a paper and a presentation on a specific aspect of Deep AI, Machine Learning, ANN, etc. The paper should cite at least 3 reputable sources. Compare and contrast to what has been stated in this book.

b) <u>Assignment for the Self-Driving Car topic</u>: Research and prepare a paper and Self-Driving Cars. Cite at least 3 reputable sources and analyze the characterizations. Compare and contrast to what has been stated in this book.

c) <u>Assignment for a Business topic</u>: Research and prepare a paper and a presentation on businesses and advanced technology. What is hot, and what is not? Cite at least 3 reputable sources. Compare and contrast to the depictions in this book.

d) <u>Assignment to do a Startup:</u> Have the students prepare a paper about how they might startup a business in this realm. They must submit a sound Business Plan for the startup. They could also be asked to present their Business Plan and so should also have a presentation deck to coincide with it.

You can certainly adjust the aforementioned assignments to fit to your particular needs and the class structure. You'll notice that I ask for 3 reputable cited sources for the paper writing based assignments. I usually steer students toward "reputable" publications, since otherwise they will cite some oddball source that has no credentials other than that they happened to write something and post it onto the Internet. You can define "reputable" in whatever way you prefer, for example some faculty think Wikipedia is not reputable while others believe it is reputable and allow students to cite it.

The reason that I usually ask for at least 3 citations is that if the student only does one or two citations they usually settle on whatever they happened to find the fastest. By requiring three citations, it usually seems to force them to look around, explore, and end-up probably finding five or more, and then whittling it down to 3 that they will actually use.

I have not specified the length of their papers, and leave that to you to tell the students what you prefer. For each of those assignments, you could end-up with a short one to two pager, or you could do a dissertation length paper. Base the length on whatever best fits for your class, and the credit amount of the assignment within the context of the other grading metrics you'll be using for the class.

I mention in the assignments that they are to do a paper and prepare a presentation. I usually try to get students to present their work. This is a good practice for what they will do in the business world. Most of the time, they will be required to prepare an analysis and present it. If you don't have the class time or inclination to have the students present, then you can of course cut out the aspect of them putting together a presentation.

If you want to point students toward highly ranked journals in AI, here's a list of the top journals as reported by *various citation counts sources* (this list changes year to year):

- o   Communications of the ACM
- o   Artificial Intelligence
- o   Cognitive Science
- o   IEEE Transactions on Pattern Analysis and Machine Intelligence
- o   Foundations and Trends in Machine Learning
- o   Journal of Memory and Language
- o   Cognitive Psychology
- o   Neural Networks
- o   IEEE Transactions on Neural Networks and Learning Systems
- o   IEEE Intelligent Systems
- o   Knowledge-based Systems

GUIDE TO USING THE CHAPTERS

For each of the chapters, I provide next some various ways to use the chapter material. You can assign the tasks as individual homework assignments, or the tasks can be used with team projects for the class. You can easily layout a series of assignments, such as indicating that the students are to do item "a" below for say Chapter 1, then "b" for the next chapter of the book, and so on.

a) What is the main point of the chapter and describe in your own words the significance of the topic,

b) Identify at least two aspects in the chapter that you agree with, and support your concurrence by providing at least one other outside researched item as support; make sure to explain your basis for disagreeing with the aspects,

c) Identify at least two aspects in the chapter that you disagree with, and support your disagreement by providing at least one other outside researched item as support; make sure to explain your basis for disagreeing with the aspects,

d) Find an aspect that was not covered in the chapter, doing so by conducting outside research, and then explain how that aspect ties into the chapter and what significance it brings to the topic,

e) Interview a specialist in industry about the topic of the chapter, collect from them their thoughts and opinions, and readdress the chapter by citing your source and how they compared and contrasted to the material,

f) Interview a relevant academic professor or researcher in a college or university about the topic of the chapter, collect from them their thoughts and opinions, and readdress the chapter by citing your source and how they compared and contrasted to the material,

g) Try to update a chapter by finding out the latest on the topic, and ascertain whether the issue or topic has now been solved or whether it is still being addressed, explain what you come up with.

The above are all ways in which you can get the students of your class involved in considering the material of a given chapter. You could mix things up by having one of those above assignments per each week, covering the chapters over the course of the semester or quarter.

As a reminder, here are the chapters of the book and you can select whichever chapters you find most valued for your particular class:

Chapter Title

1   Eliot Framework for AI Self-Driving Cars

2   Regulatory Scapegoating and AI Self-Driving Cars

3   Trust Beliefs and AI Self-Driving Cars

4   Post-Pandemic Era and AI Self-Driving Cars

5   Debating The Future and AI Self-Driving Cars

6   Purposeless Driving and AI Self-Driving Cars

7   AI Dimwitted Trickery and AI Self-Driving Cars

8   Dangerous Roads and AI Self-Driving Cars

9   UFO Videos and AI Self-Driving Cars

10   AI Cannot Be An Inventor and AI Self-Driving Cars

11   AI Benefiting Humanity and AI Self-Driving Cars

Companion Book By This Author

Advances in AI and Autonomous Vehicles: Cybernetic Self-Driving Cars

Practical Advances in Artificial Intelligence (AI) and Machine Learning
by
Dr. Lance B. Eliot, MBA, PhD

This title is available via Amazon and other book sellers

Companion Book By This Author

Self-Driving Cars: "The Mother of All AI Projects"

by Dr. Lance B. Eliot, MBA, PhD

This title is available via Amazon and other book seller

Innovation and Thought Leadership on Self-Driving Driverless Cars

by Dr. Lance B. Eliot, MBA, PhD

This title is available via Amazon and other book sellers

This title is available via Amazon and other book sellers

Companion Book By This Author

Introduction to
Driverless Self-Driving Cars

by Dr. Lance B. Eliot, MBA, PhD

This title is available via Amazon and other book sellers

Companion Book By This Author

Autonomous Vehicle Driverless Self-Driving Cars and Artificial Intelligence

by Dr. Lance B. Eliot, MBA, PhD

This title is available via Amazon and other book sellers

Companion Book By This Author

Transformative Artificial Intelligence Driverless Self-Driving Cars

by Dr. Lance B. Eliot, MBA, PhD

This title is available via Amazon and other book sellers

Companion Book By This Author

Disruptive Artificial Intelligence and Driverless Self-Driving Cars

by Dr. Lance B. Eliot, MBA, PhD

Chapter Title

This title is available via Amazon and other book sellers

Companion Book By This Author

State-of-the-Art
AI Driverless Self-Driving Cars

by Dr. Lance B. Eliot, MBA, PhD

This title is available via Amazon and other book sellers

This title is available via Amazon and other book sellers

This title is available via Amazon and other book sellers

Companion Book By This Author

Crucial Advances for
AI Self-Driving Cars

by Dr. Lance B. Eliot, MBA, PhD

This title is available via Amazon and other book sellers

Companion Book By This Author

Sociotechnical Insights and AI Driverless Cars

by Dr. Lance B. Eliot, MBA, PhD

This title is available via Amazon and other book sellers

This title is available via Amazon and other book sellers

This title is available via Amazon and other book sellers

**The Cutting Edge of
AI Autonomous Cars**

by Dr. Lance B. Eliot, MBA, PhD

Chapter Title

This title is available via Amazon and other book sellers

<u>Companion Book By This Author</u>

The Next Wave of
AI Self-Driving Cars

by Dr. Lance B. Eliot, MBA, PhD

<u>Chapter Title</u>

This title is available via Amazon and other book sellers

<u>Companion Book By This Author</u>

Revolutionary Innovations of AI Self-Driving Cars

by Dr. Lance B. Eliot, MBA, PhD

<u>Chapter Title</u>

1   Eliot Framework for AI Self-Driving Cars

2   Exascale Supercomputer and AI Self-Driving Cars

3   Superhuman AI and AI Self-Driving Cars

4   Olfactory e-Nose Sensors and AI Self-Driving Cars

5   Perpetual Computing and AI Self-Driving Cars

6   Byzantine Generals Problem and AI Self-Driving Cars

7   Driver Traffic Guardians and AI Self-Driving Cars

8   Anti-Gridlock Laws and AI Self-Driving Cars

9   Arguing Machines and AI Self-Driving Cars

This title is available via Amazon and other book sellers

Companion Book By This Author

AI Self-Driving Cars
Breakthroughs

by Dr. Lance B. Eliot, MBA, PhD

Chapter Title

This title is available via Amazon and other book sellers

<u>Companion Book By This Author</u>

Trailblazing Trends for
AI Self-Driving Cars

by Dr. Lance B. Eliot, MBA, PhD

<u>Chapter Title</u>

This title is available via Amazon and other book sellers

Companion Book By This Author

Ingenious Strides for
AI Driverless Cars

by Dr. Lance B. Eliot, MBA, PhD

This title is available via Amazon and other book sellers

<u>Companion Book By This Author</u>

AI Self-Driving Cars
Inventiveness

by Dr. Lance B. Eliot, MBA, PhD

<u>Chapter Title</u>

This title is available via Amazon and other book sellers

Visionary Secrets of AI Driverless Cars

by Dr. Lance B. Eliot, MBA, PhD

Chapter Title

This title is available via Amazon and other book sellers

Spearheading
AI Self-Driving Cars

by Dr. Lance B. Eliot, MBA, PhD

Chapter Title

1   Eliot Framework for AI Self-Driving Cars

2   Artificial Pain and AI Self-Driving Cars

3   Stop-and-Frisks and AI Self-Driving Cars

4   Cars Careening and AI Self-Driving Cars

5   Sounding Out Car Noises and AI Self-Driving Cars

6   No Speed Limit Autobahn and AI Self-Driving Car

7   Noble Cause Corruption and AI Self-Driving Cars

8   AI Rockstars and AI Self-Driving Cars

**This title is available via Amazon and other book sellers**

Companion Book By This Author

Spurring
AI Self-Driving Cars

by Dr. Lance B. Eliot, MBA, PhD

This title is available via Amazon and other book sellers

Companion Book By This Author

Avant-Garde
AI Driverless Cars

by Dr. Lance B. Eliot, MBA, PhD

Chapter Title

This title is available via Amazon and other book sellers

Companion Book By This Author

AI Self-Driving Cars
Evolvement

by Dr. Lance B. Eliot, MBA, PhD

Chapter Title

This title is available via Amazon and other book sellers

<u>Companion Book By This Author</u>

AI Driverless Cars
Chrysalis

by Dr. Lance B. Eliot, MBA, PhD

<u>Chapter Title</u>

This title is available via Amazon and other book sellers

Companion Book By This Author

Boosting
AI Autonomous Cars

by Dr. Lance B. Eliot, MBA, PhD

Chapter Title

This title is available via Amazon and other book sellers

AI Self-Driving Cars
Trendsetting

by Dr. Lance B. Eliot, MBA, PhD

This title is available via Amazon and other book sellers

Companion Book By This Author

AI Autonomous Cars
Forefront

by Dr. Lance B. Eliot, MBA, PhD

This title is available via Amazon and other book sellers

Companion Book By This Author

AI Autonomous Cars
Emergence

by Dr. Lance B. Eliot, MBA, PhD

This title is available via Amazon and other book sellers

Companion Book By This Author

AI Autonomous Cars Progress

by Dr. Lance B. Eliot, MBA, PhD

<u>Chapter Title</u>

This title is available via Amazon and other book sellers

Companion Book By This Author

AI Self-Driving Cars Prognosis

by Dr. Lance B. Eliot, MBA, PhD

This title is available via Amazon and other book sellers

<u>Companion Book By This Author</u>

AI Self-Driving Cars
Momentum

by Dr. Lance B. Eliot, MBA, PhD

<u>Chapter Title</u>

This title is available via Amazon and other book sellers

<u>Companion Book By This Author</u>

AI Self-Driving Cars
Headway
by Dr. Lance B. Eliot, MBA, PhD

<u>Chapter Title</u>

This title is available via Amazon and other book sellers

<u>Companion Book By This Author</u>

AI Self-Driving Cars
Vicissitude

by Dr. Lance B. Eliot, MBA, PhD

<u>Chapter Title</u>

This title is available via Amazon and other book sellers

Companion Book By This Author

AI Self-Driving Cars
Autonomy

by Dr. Lance B. Eliot, MBA, PhD

This title is available via Amazon and other book sellers

Companion Book By This Author

AI Driverless Cars
Transmutation

by Dr. Lance B. Eliot, MBA, PhD

This title is available via Amazon and other book sellers

<u>Companion Book By This Author</u>

AI Driverless Cars
Potentiality

by Dr. Lance B. Eliot, MBA, PhD

<u>Chapter Title</u>

1   Eliot Framework for AI Self-Driving Cars

2   Russian Values and AI Self-Driving Cars

3   Friendships Uplift and AI Self-Driving Cars

4   Dogs Driving and AI Self-Driving Cars

5   Hypodermic Needles and AI Self-Driving Cars

6   Sharing Self-Driving Tech Is Not Likely

7   Uber Driver "Kidnapper" Is Self-Driving Car Lesson

8   Gender Driving Biases In AI Self-Driving Cars

9   Slain Befriended Dolphins Are Self-Driving Car Lesson

10   Analysis Of AI In Government Report

11 Mobility Frenzy and AI Self-Driving Cars

This title is available via Amazon and other book sellers

Companion Book By This Author

AI Driverless Cars
Realities

by Dr. Lance B. Eliot, MBA, PhD

Chapter Title

This title is available via Amazon and other book sellers

Companion Book By This Author

**AI Self-Driving Cars
Materiality**

by Dr. Lance B. Eliot, MBA, PhD

Chapter Title

This title is available via Amazon and other book sellers

Companion Book By This Author

AI Self-Driving Cars
Accordance

by Dr. Lance B. Eliot, MBA, PhD

<u>Chapter Title</u>

1 Eliot Framework for AI Self-Driving Cars

2 Regulatory Scapegoating and AI Self-Driving Cars

3 Trust Beliefs and AI Self-Driving Cars

4 Post-Pandemic Era and AI Self-Driving Cars

5 Debating The Future and AI Self-Driving Cars

6 Purposeless Driving and AI Self-Driving Cars

7 AI Dimwitted Trickery and AI Self-Driving Cars

8 Dangerous Roads and AI Self-Driving Cars

9 UFO Videos and AI Self-Driving Cars

10 AI Cannot Be An Inventor and AI Self-Driving Cars

11 AI Benefiting Humanity and AI Self-Driving Cars

This title is available via Amazon and other book sellers

ABOUT THE AUTHOR

Dr. Lance B. Eliot, Ph.D., MBA is a globally recognized AI expert and thought leader, an experienced executive and leader, a successful serial entrepreneur, and a noted scholar on AI, including that his Forbes and AI Trends columns have amassed over 2.8+ million views, his books on AI are frequently ranked in the Top 10 of all-time AI books, his journal articles are widely cited, and he has developed and fielded dozens of AI systems.

He currently serves as the CEO of Techbruim, Inc. and has over twenty years of industry experience including serving as a corporate officer in billion-dollar sized firms and was a partner in a major consulting firm. He is also a successful entrepreneur having founded, ran, and sold several high-tech related businesses.

Dr. Eliot previously hosted the popular radio show *Technotrends* that was also available on American Airlines flights via their in-flight audio program, he has made appearances on CNN, has been a frequent speaker at industry conferences, and his podcasts have been downloaded over 100,000 times.

A former professor at the University of Southern California (USC), he founded and led an innovative research lab on Artificial Intelligence. He also previously served on the faculty of the University of California Los Angeles (UCLA) and was a visiting professor at other major universities. He was elected to the International Board of the Society for Information Management (SIM), a prestigious association of over 3,000 high-tech executives worldwide.

He has performed extensive community service, including serving as Senior Science Adviser to the Congressional Vice-Chair of the Congressional Committee on Science & Technology. He has served on the Board of the OC Science & Engineering Fair (OCSEF), where he is also has been a Grand Sweepstakes judge, and likewise served as a judge for the Intel International SEF (ISEF). He served as the Vice-Chair of the Association for Computing Machinery (ACM) Chapter, a prestigious association of computer scientists. Dr. Eliot has been a shark tank judge for the USC Mark Stevens Center for Innovation on start-up pitch competitions and served as a mentor for several incubators and accelerators in Silicon Valley and in Silicon Beach.

Dr. Eliot holds a Ph.D. from USC, MBA, and Bachelor's in Computer Science, and earned the CDP, CCP, CSP, CDE, and CISA certifications.

ADDENDUM

AI Self-Driving Cars Accordance

Practical Advances in Artificial Intelligence (AI) and Machine Learning

By

Dr. Lance B. Eliot, MBA, PhD

––––––––

For supplemental materials of this book, visit:

www.ai-selfdriving-cars.guru

For special orders of this book, contact:

LBE Press Publishing

Email: LBE.Press.Publishing@gmail.com

www.ingramcontent.com/pod-product-compliance
Lightning Source LLC
Chambersburg PA
CBHW052140070326
40690CB00047B/1200